REBEL COACH

REBEL COACH
My Football Family
By John Vaught

Memphis State University Press, Memphis

Editor's Note

Johnny Vaught coached college football—taught it about as well as any man who ever lived. It is unlikely that the nation ever again will see a football fiefdom quite like the one Vaught built at Ole Miss. As I edited the manuscript I understood the football program at the University of Mississippi for the first time. I learned how Vaught turned a loser into a winner. Even to a Mississippi State alumnus, such as I, Vaught's memoirs have a warmth and charm you associate with big southern families. His book is a welcome contribution to the literature of college football.

William W. Sorrels
Managing Editor
The Commercial Appeal
Memphis, Tennessee

The Vaught Years

The Nation's Top 10 Coaches with 15 Seasons or More
And Active in 1970

Coach	Won	Lost	Tied	Pct.*
Darrell Royal, Texas	135	42	4	76.2
JOHN VAUGHT, Ole Miss	185	58	12	76.1
Woody Hayes, Ohio State	167	54	7	75.6
Bob Blackman, Darthmouth	150	49	8	75.3
Dan Devine, Missouri	119	41	8	74.3
Ara Parseghian, Notre Dame	133	51	6	72.3
Paul Bryant, Alabama	199	66	16	71.3
Ben Schwartzwalder, Syracuse	167	76	2	68.7
John Yovicsin, Harvard	110	53	5	67.5
Ralph Jordan, Auburn	137	66	5	67.4

*Based on wins - losses

National Championship

Ole Miss — 1960
(Awarded Look-Grantland Rice Trophy by vote of FWAA)

SEC Championships
(Since 1947)

School	Won	Tied
Ole Miss	6	0
Alabama	3	2
Georgia	3	1
Tennessee	3	1
LSU	2	1
Georgia Tech	1	1
Tulane	1	0
Kentucky	1	0
Auburn	1	0
Mississippi State	0	0
Florida	0	0
Vanderbilt	0	0

Ole Miss' championship years: 1947, 1954, 1955, 1960, 1962, 1963

Ole Miss' Bowl Record

(1947-1971)

Year	Bowl	PF	PA	Opponent
1948	Delta	13	9	TCU
1953	Sugar	7	24	Georgia Tech
1955	Sugar	0	21	Navy
1956	Cotton	14	13	TCU
1958	Sugar	39	7	Texas
1958	Gator	7	3	Florida
1960	Sugar	21	0	LSU
1961	Sugar	14	6	Rice
1962	Cotton	7	12	Texas
1963	Sugar	17	13	Arkansas
1964	Sugar	7	12	Alabama
1964	Bluebonnet	7	14	Tulsa
1965	Liberty	13	7	Auburn
1966	Bluebonnet	0	19	Texas
1967	Sun	7	14	Texas-El Paso
1968	Liberty	34	17	Virginia Tech
1970	Sugar	27	22	Arkansas
1971	Gator	28	35	Auburn

Won 10, Lost 8

Ole Miss holds national record for consecutive bowl games — 14.

VIII

LIST OF PHOTOGRAPHS

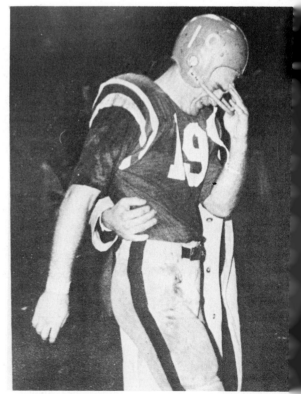

CONTENTS

Introduction

Every coach at one time or another has wanted to be a Monday morning quarterback. I stood on the sidelines for 35 years in Texas, North Carolina and Mississippi, but I intend to step up on my own soapbox in these recollections. When it comes to Ole Miss football I have viewpoints that have been building in my mind since I first saw Oxford in 1946.

Everyone is welcome to his opinion of Ole Miss, which is at Oxford—the fictional Jefferson of William Faulkner, but just home to me. Tom Siler of the *Knoxville News-Sentinel* said a coach once told him:

"I've got an idea what hell is like; I coached at Ole Miss for a few years."

Well, one of us confused heaven and hell. And who is the luckier man? Happiness means a lot to me, and I found it at Ole Miss in a football family, my statewide family. At times I feel like a proud grandfather when I think about my teams. My life began on a hard rock Texas ranch, but my recollections must begin at the University of Mississippi. My goal in this book is a simple one: to present a clear picture of Ole Miss football since 1946. I intend to be honest and reveal the planning involving football triumphs without whitewashing the mistakes behind my defeats. Anything less would be a mockery to my players. Where cheers are due, I want my boys to hear them. When the shoe begins to pinch, I want the cry to be mine.

I saw Mississippi boys climb a football mountain in the south. They won—and won big—at a school many experts considered too small and too isolated ever to be a winner. The accomplishments of my Mississippians revive memories of Glenn "Pop" Warner, who coached tiny Carlisle in Pennsylvania to national acclaim in the early part of this century. Pop never forgot that it was his Indians—Jim Thorpe, Redwater and the others—who loved to win and hated to lose. I feel the same way about my Rebels.

John H. Vaught
Oxford, Mississippi
1971

1

Mississippi Mystique

Each December a man in Arkansas sends me a Christmas card. He wants to haunt me, not wish me Merry Christmas. The man draws slanted goal posts on the back of the card. I understand. He doesn't want me to forget something I learned a long time ago: football fans have long memories. There are some games they never forget. To his dying day, I'm sure, my pen pal in Arkansas will say the 1960 Ole Miss-Arkansas game should have gone into the books as a 7-7 tie.

But it didn't. The story goes back to October 22, 1960, to a game people on both sides of the Mississippi River still talk about.

There are three seconds remaining and 40,000 people in War Memorial Stadium in Little Rock are standing and screaming. In our bench area, some boys are turning their eyes away from the field; others watch with a stare. A few are praying. In the stands every eye is glued to Jake Gibbs, whose hands are out for the snap, and Allen Green, who is ready to try for the winning field goal. Referee Tommy Bell swings his arm to start the clock. Our center, Fred Lentjes, puts the ball right in Gibbs' hands. Green, a senior trying for his first three-pointer, moves forward and kicks the ball 39 yards. Bell throws up both hands, signalling it good. The scoreboard lights show: Ole Miss 10, Arkansas 7. The clock reads: 00:00.

Actually, Green kicked the three points twice. With 16 seconds remaining he split the goal posts, but Bell, now an official in the National Football League, had whistled a time out before the snap. Arkansas fans, who thought fate had smiled for them, went wild, and rightly so. I was uptight myself, but a lot of things were running through my mind. We had made a first down on the Arkansas 18 with 25 seconds left. I sent a pass play in to Gibbs, our quarterback. I wanted a touchdown, but I knew if we missed on an incompletion the clock would stop and give us time to try for a field goal. But Gibbs, who was one fine football player, was rushed. He couldn't get the pass away and Ole Miss took a short loss. We had no time-outs left and we could have looked pretty silly. So, that last-second field goal—the one that counted—was an awfully big play.

To this day, the game is not lightly discussed in Arkansas. The Razorback's fine young coach, Frank Broyles, took the loss pretty hard.

"The referee gave it to them because he had blown the whistle on the down before and the first kick was good," he told newsmen after the game. "I've never been beaten by a field goal that wasn't good. Everybody in the park knew it wasn't good."

I thought it was, but you can't tell from the sidelines. Green, who put it in the air, said it was. Gibbs, a lot like Charley Conerly when it comes to talking—which means both are just the opposite of blabbermouths—said only, "It went through all right." I think Tommy Bell defended his call with an excellent choice of words: "If it hadn't been good I wouldn't have called it good."

The controversial kick had several sequels. Up in the press

box, sports writers were busy filing their stories when an Arkansas supporter rushed in waving a football. "I was sitting in the end zone and caught that kick," he shouted, "and I'll kill any son-of-a-bitch who says that kick was good." One newsman admitted to me later that not one single writer argued with the excited gentleman, who was finally ushered out. I don't think he's the man who sends the Christmas cards.

Green's kick brought one of the biggest wins in Ole Miss history. It helped earn us the *Look* magazine–Grantland Rice Trophy, the first time a southern team had won that symbol of a national championship by vote of the Football Writers Association of America. In the wire service polls Coach Murray Warmath's Minnesota Gophers edged us out as No. 1, but the FWAA honor clearly revealed that Mississippi football rated with the best in the land. A year earlier, in 1959, Ole Miss had finished second in all the major polls. That time, Coach Ben Schwartzwalder's Syracuse team narrowly nosed us out. It may well be asked, and I have often thought about it myself, how Ole Miss, a small university in one of the poorest states, became a football power.

Record books, at best cold and impersonal logs of human endeavor, show that my Mississippians won 185 games, lost 58 and tied 12 between 1947 and 1970. In those years—my time as a head coach and a period that saw student enrollment grow from 2,000 to 7,800—they won, in addition to a national championship, six Southeastern Conference titles and played in 18 bowl games. The last 14 bowl games came consecutively and established a national record.

The truth about football at the University of Mississippi must be searched out beyond newspaper headlines, telecasts and a quarter century of statistics. It might be argued, perhaps even charged, that money made Mississippi football. But if success went to the highest bidder, Ole Miss would be an also ran. The richer schools would clobber us with ease.

For the 1970-71 school year our athletic budget totaled $982,000, which includes funds for all sports and must be self-sustaining. Anything that costs close to a million dollars is big business to me, but many schools in the Southeastern Conference have larger budgets. Tennessee has a fine program and a 2.2 million dollar budget. By way of comparison, Ohio State University, in the powerful Big Ten Conference, has an athletic budget exceeding 3 million dollars.

Outside athletics, the University of Mississippi operated on a 26 million-dollar budget in 1970-71. That is a 20 million-dollar jump since 1946, but the school needed every penny of it, and more. I think it is good that the Ole Miss athletic department must rise or fall on its own financial ledgers, which have managed to stay in the black since 1946 when the budget was $250,000.

I wanted to win each game I coached and I have searched the state for the super-athlete to make it possible. But I told each boy who signed with us that his education came first. Professional teams drafted nine boys from my 1970 squad, but I never thought of Ole Miss as a football factory for the pros. Over the years, most of the boys have gone on to other fields, just about any you can name from medicine to engineering. Three became Rhodes Scholars.

After the 1971 Gator Bowl our athletic department was able to give $10,000 to the university library. It could be argued that this money belonged to the school in the first place, but the point is that football is helping to buy books for young Mississippians. If the athletic department took a million dollars from the university's operating or academic budget, I would recommend curtailment or abandonment of intercollegiate athletics.

The athletic department shares in bookstore and Student Union soft drink concession profits, but most of its funds come from a single source—football tickets. In seeking athletes from 465 Mississippi public schools and a handful of private academies, Ole Miss doesn't have a slush fund or a Lear Jet at its disposal. There have to be other reasons for its football success.

Perhaps a letter written by a University of Tennessee

alumnus to a Mississippi friend after Ole Miss' 38 to 0 upset of Tennessee on November 15, 1969, can be used as a starter for my analysis.

November 16, 1969
Bartlett, Tennessee

Dear Willie:

Did you ever hear of a Mississippian who despised Ole Miss? Have they nothing else in the state to be proud of? Just what is the mystique which makes a Rebel fan in Madison, Wisconsin, wire me after a Tennessee defeat when I never ever rode his donkey during the years Ole Miss couldn't win? Is it mystique which makes great players of Mississippi schoolboys who couldn't have had all that good coaching in high school? I know most of the players come from little ole crossroads farm towns, and that they're big and strong and all that, but how in the hell does Vaught manage to make All-Americans out of them when they've probably never heard of a post pattern except on TV? Is it true that Vaught makes more money than a Rockefeller? Do I hate Ole Miss more than I should?

Sincerely,
Ed

Few $28,500-a-year football coaches get to meet a Rockefeller. For many years now, I have felt that a mutual bond united the football players who come to Ole Miss. The fact that I relied primarily on home-state athletes has to be considered significant since it is the boys, not the coaches, who put Ole Miss alongside Oklahoma and Texas as the three "winningest" teams of the past 25 years. My assistants and I were happy to help sew the thread of pride we saw into the image of a winner. When it was fourth and three with time running out I knew I could count on my Mississippians to dig a little deeper.

The boys were never bigger than life. They came to us from Noxapater, Redwood, Benoit and a hundred other little towns in the hills, piney woods and Delta, joining with cousins from Jackson, Tupelo, Greenville, Clarksdale, Gulfport and other larger cities. Practically all of them grew up in rural or small town traditions, but they were alert, intelligent and highly aware of the world around them. Family tradition meant a lot to them, but they read *Sports Illustrated,* not *Confederate Veteran* magazine. I suspect one of the intangibles in Ole Miss football begins with an understanding of Mississippians. That raises the question of which Mississippians I have in mind, the state's 1,393,283 whites or 815,770 blacks.

My answer is both, for while my teams at Ole Miss were all-white this picture will change rapidly in the future. Segregation was legal nationally until May 17, 1954, when the United States Supreme Court handed down its historic decision, but color barriers remained in Mississippi colleges until September 10, 1962, when Justice Hugo Black upheld a circuit court ruling and said Ole Miss must admit black students. A riot 20 days later shaped an image of our university as a last citadel of white supremacy, and this legacy has cost us some black athletes. In 1970 one of the nation's most sought after black quarterbacks declined to visit Ole Miss but signed a grant-in-aid with Mississippi State. I have had conferences with Department of Health, Education and Welfare people, and I acknowledge that I may have dragged my feet from time to time. I also see a new era of racial amity evolving in Mississippi in the years ahead.

In the past it was difficult to grow up in Mississippi, whether white or black, without developing a defensive or apprehensive attitude. Even in 1970 whites and blacks alike bore the cross of a per capita annual income of $2,218, but it must be remembered that 20 years ago it was only $755. In books and on the air Mississippi boys learn they are last in just about all statistical categories. I may be stepping in over my head, but this is the material that helps the meek to rise up and conquer.

Pride often is the difference. College football has become an outlet, a gateway to recognition for a people whose historians tell them that Mississippi's per capita income was fifth highest in the nation until the Civil War and resulting hard times beset the state.

But it is the modern era that concerns us here, and after 1954 white Mississippians tried to preserve the caste system they inherited. As the years wore on they felt they were looked upon, more and more, with scorn. Events occurred which meant little to outsiders but were of great importance to Mississippians. In 1959 and 1960 girls from Ole Miss went to Atlantic City and won back-to-back Miss America titles. Here were moonlight and magnolia—traditional Southern beauty triumphant. Most of all, it was recognition. Meanwhile, Ole Miss football teams reached an uncommonly high plateau, including a national championship in 1960.

I do not pretend that the Mississippi mystique, if there is such a thing, can be explained satisfactorily by a football coach who is a Mississippian by choice, not birth. I can say with certainty that I learned early in my years at Ole Miss not to underestimate the pride of my Mississippians. I have sketched only my impressions here; the roots of Mississippi mystique rest in the deep furrow of history and I leave that to others.

I know without any doubt whatsoever that Ole Miss football is more of a family affair than at any other institution in the country. Our recruiting in the state begins in the cradle and continues until the boys put on their cleats. Men who played on my first Rebel team a quarter of a century ago—John H. Bowen, Dave Bridgers, Will Glover and Will Webb—have sent sons back for me to coach. I first saw some of my players when they came to Ole Miss games holding their fathers' hands. One boy, Bo Bowen, a fine senior fullback on my 1969 team, had his picture made in my office when he wore diapers.

Watson Spoelstra of the *Detroit News* saw Jim Poole catch a pass in 1969 and told his Michigan readers about Ole Miss' "good blood lines." He used those words because Jim's father, Buster Poole, coached my defensive line. It seems only yesterday that Buster's brother, Barney Poole, teamed with Charley Conerly to set national passing records in 1947. But more than records stick out in my mind. In the

Chattanooga game that year, Barney caught eight straight passes, then had his breath knocked out by a hard tackle. After he was down a few seconds, Buster ran out on the field.

"You hurt, Barney?" he asked.

"Naw, I'm just tired." When Barney grinned, Buster blew up. "Well, dammit, get up! It don't look good. You know mama's sitting up there in the stands. If you don't get up she's going to be down here in a few minutes."

Through the years, there have been 30 sets of football brothers at Ole Miss. In the 1940's, there were five Pooles— brothers and cousins from Route 3, Gloster—on the squad at the same time. There is a family atmosphere at Ole Miss, and across the state.

Family pride and dedication by good athletes enabled Ole Miss to enjoy success, with only one losing season in the last twenty-four. College football is an exceptionally emotional matter, and our supporters as well as players share it. I saw a good example of it during our 1958 Gator Bowl game with Florida in Jacksonville. Our fullback, Charlie Flowers, got a lick on the head. Doc Varner, the team physician, took a look and said, "Charlie, I've got to get you to a hospital."

Doc had noticed a slight amount of blood on the outside of Flowers' eye. Charlie was confused, but Doc got him into the dressing room under the stadium. In a little while, Charlie snapped out of it. Then he heard cheering outside. His eyes wide with alarm, he looked at Varner and said, "Doc, I'm going to die."

Varner shook his head, trying to assure Charlie that he was going to be all right. Charlie remained unconvinced. "I don't know, Doc."

"Why, Charlie?"

"Well," Flowers said, "Ole Miss is out there playing football and you're in here with me."

Every athlete at Ole Miss understands how Charlie felt. Doc, a 1928 graduate, symbolizes a Mississippian's dedication to the team. He never misses a game and wore the same brown hat to each game for 21 years. Such are the football attitudes—call it mystique—that bind Ole Miss to family and state. It was my good fortune to become a part of it.

2

Long Ago
And Far Away

In 1954 the postmaster in Trezevant, a west Tennessee town of 944 people, sent a postcard to Britt Rogers in Tupelo, Mississippi. He said Ole Miss might want to talk to a 6-1, 210-pound prospect up there. Britt, an Ole Miss man, got word to me and I sent our recruiter, Tom Swayze, and Junie Hovious, an assistant coach, up to take a look. The boy didn't live in Trezevant, but out in the county. The farther Tom and Junie drove the narrower the road got. Just before the road bumped into a clump of oaks, they came to a house with a huge shade tree in the front yard. A big farm boy strolled out on the porch. Immediately, Junie elbowed Tom and said, "If that's the one, let's take him."

Tom signed the boy to a scholarship on the porch a few minutes later, although he prefers to see a boy play first. But everything turned out all right. The big kid was Gene Hickerson, now an All-Pro guard who has been leading such runners as Jimmy Brown and Leroy Kelly on Cleveland sweeps for a dozen years.

When such boys show up at Ole Miss, I see myself as a boy once again. It is easy for me to identify with their ambitions. I was fourteen before I saw my first football game, a high school contest at the county fair in Graham, back in Young County, Texas. The game didn't really set me on fire, but I liked it. I thought the boys were having a lot of fun. I didn't realize that one day I would have an opportunity to play football. In those days my life revolved around farming and ranching.

I was born on May 6, 1909, in a two-story, T-shaped frame ranch house three miles outside Ingleside, Texas. And I was never lonely; my family was a large one. I was the sixth of eleven children born to Rufus and Sally Harris Vaught. My world seemed big enough and happy enough. I had two brothers and three sisters older than I and three brothers and two sisters younger. Our parents struggled to provide for us on a section of land—640 acres—in the northern part of Young County. Nature made the going tough, with the countryside filled with the usual mesquite, scrub oaks and cactus. A cow had to hustle to find grass, and the farmers and ranchers could be proud when they made a go of it. Most of them built character rather than estates, but I did not realize that as a boy. If the Vaught family was poor, it never occurred to me. I guess that was one of the major blessings of the old days.

Farm life was a real family affair. The boys handled the usual chores. My brothers and I chopped stove wood to feed the big Kalamazoo my mother used to bake wonderful loaves of bread. There's no smell quite like an oven full of baking dough. I remember the cold winter nights I followed my father and his swinging lantern down to the barn to check on the stock. I never knew a farmer who didn't hate winter. Even in winter, though, everyone seemed to have something to do. In the house my mother and my sisters usually kept the sewing machine going. We didn't stay up late at night, but after supper we sat by coal oil lamps and read our school lessons. It was under those conditions that I began to build a certain appreciation for good books and serious study.

We had our share of games and toys as children. I remember clearly the little red wagon that all of us pulled around the yard. When I was four years old one of my brothers was pulling me in the wagon when it turned over. I tumbled out and fell face down on the jagged edge of a tin can. My parents didn't take me to a doctor—the closest one was in Olney, ten miles to the northeast—but they did their best with home remedies. I think they soaked the wound in coal oil, and maybe a little turpentine was used. The accident left a two-inch diagonal scar on my right cheek that stands out rather vividly. It's the kind of scar that makes little farm girls turn around in the desks at school and grin at you and say, "I wonder what you looked like, Johnny, before the horse kicked you."

Hardworking and religious, my family was typical of those in Young and Jack counties in the first quarter of this century. My father was of North German ancestry; my mother was English. For all the families living nearby, Ingleside served as the social center. It had a church, a parsonage, a general store and a square brick building everyone called the schoolhouse. I thought it was a good school and I liked all the teachers. It didn't matter to me that our farm was three miles away and we had to get to school the best way we could. My father let me ride Prince, a big sorrel horse, to school. I stabled him there in a long wooden shed.

Out in Texas, you learn early about a Norther, a wind that whistles in from the north suddenly and without warning in the winter. I can remember riding Prince to school in the morning in mild weather and galloping home in the afternoon in a bone-chilled condition. It was nothing for temperatures to drop thirty degrees in a couple of hours. There was a saying that the only thing between Ingleside and the North Pole when a Norther struck was a single strand of barbed wire. The older and wiser cowboys said even it had been cut, probably at Amarillo.

Ingleside school didn't have football, but the kids played a lot of basketball. I began playing basketball when I was thirteen or fourteen and our team would go around the county playing other schools. We usually did well. I think being on the basketball team helped me to adjust quickly to football in Fort Worth.

With completion of the eighth grade at Ingleside, I was undecided about going on to school elsewhere or going to work. I was fifteen, an age at which a lot of boys went to work fulltime in those days. "Ellie," Elbert Vaught, my oldest brother, lived in Olney and when I heard he and his wife planned to drive down to Fort Worth I decided to go with them. I had no idea of what I could do, except stay with my maternal grandmother, Mrs. Madeline Gertrude Harris, at 3410 Millett Avenue. It was a spur of the moment decision, but I had visited in Fort Worth from time to time with my family.

Ingleside is about one hundred road miles to the northwest of Fort Worth, but the real distance between it and my farm world was much greater. If Fort Worth was a "Cow Town" in 1925 I failed to recognize it. The creak of a wagon wheel, the bellow of a young calf and the hoofbeats of a cow pony— none of those things on the farm had prepared me for the sights and sounds of a city of 150,000 people. The way people dressed fascinated me—and the way they acted. Some of them wore boots and cowboy hats, but you could tell by the way they walked that they had never ridden a horse. And they all seemed to be going some place in a hell of a hurry. Out on the ranch, I had heard the story of the man who owned the Four Deuces Ranch—won by pulling four deuces in a poker game—and I figured that was done fair and square. But the hurrying city slickers made me wary, although all I had to lose were the clothes on my back. Nightfall in a city is when a farm boy gets lonely. That's the way it was for me. I remember hearing a street car in the dead of the night and wondering what kind of a job a man could be going to when he's supposed to be sleeping. Daybreak at grandmother's house on Millett Avenue helped me to get used to Fort Worth. She had a back lot of chickens, and the crowing of an old white Leghorn rooster bridged the gap between Ingleside and my new life.

Joe Boykin helped me, too. A distant cousin, Joe had moved into Fort Worth from an east Texas farm. When I got to Fort Worth Joe was working at the Santa Fe depot. He asked me to work there too. The opportunity to become a redcap delighted me. Joe and I toted luggage and baggage all that summer. Our busiest time was between 7 and 10 p.m., when the big passenger trains came through. Once, a man tipped me five dollars. I guess he was an oilman or a wealthy merchant. When our duties were light, Joe and I would sit on baggage carts, swinging our legs and talking about the future. Working around a railroad makes you realize that those ribbons of steel that seem to come together in infinity are in reality arrows to other towns and other lives. One day, late in the summer of 1925, Joe looked at me and said, "Johnny, let's go back to school this fall. We'll keep our jobs here too."

The idea appealed to me. I told Joe that was what I would like to do. Fortunately, my grandmother and her two sons—my uncles, Edell Harris and Charles Harris—kept an eye on me. After school began they could see that I wasn't able to work at the depot and keep up with my class work. Grand-mother finally told me, "Johnny, you just live with us and help with the chores and go on to school."

My uncles also promised to help me, and the decision to go back to school has to be a turning point in my life. I worked when I could and spent many weekends at the Glen Garden Country Club caddying with Byron Nelson and other kids.

Millett Avenue is in an area on Fort Worth's southeast side called "Poly" because of Polytechnic High School, where I enrolled in the fall and began my football career. Uncle Edell encouraged me and Joe Boykin to try out for the team.

"You two country boys come over here," Coach Rube Leissner yelled at us the first day. Then he began to show us the fundamentals of blocking, which is essentially the same as tackling without arms. Looking back, I can see that Leissner was a fine man as well as a good coach. He was a disciplinarian and a good influence. I don't want to brag, but he put me on the first team the first day. Frankly, Leissner didn't have much talent to work with. I guess he just picked the biggest boys. I was about 5-11 and I must have weighed 165 pounds. But there were kids playing for Poly who weighed only a little over 100 pounds. There was one little guy in that category named Jack Newell. He could taunt another team to death.

My first game in 1925 opened my eyes. It was a disaster. We played against the Masonic Home, an orphans home, in Fort Worth. The kids at the home, out on Vaughan Boulevard, had been playing together since they were eight or nine years old, and they beat our Poly team to death. They did everything they wanted to do with us. As I recall, the score was 40 to 0. My uncles were big football fans and they saw the game. "Johnny," Uncle Edell said, "you ought to be ashamed of yourself for letting those little bitty orphans beat you."

That defeat, as much as anything I can remember, instilled a desire in me to win. I have hated to lose ever since.

Back in 1925 there wasn't a great deal of emphasis on football at Poly, but I loved to play. It seemed Rube played me at just about any position—end, tackle or guard. I took my licks and fought back tears from time to time, but I enjoyed every minute of it. Speaking of tears, I guess that's why I remember Jack Newell so well. That little rascal is responsible for one of the worst physical beatings I ever took in high school.

We were playing Oak Cliff High School in Dallas when they had Father Lumpkin as their running back. In later years, Newell confessed his sins in a letter to a friends:

> Most people think of the great block that Harrison Stafford put on Vaught as the worst thing that happened to him in football, but it is not. My first year we were playing Oak Cliff High School of Dallas, and it had a man playing for them named "Father" Lumpkin, who later played at Georgia Tech.
>
> They called him "Father" because he must have been twenty-three when he was playing us that year. He was as big as a gorilla and he ran like a deer.

We were playing a six-man line. I was the center and weighed ninety-eight pounds, and was backing up the line on the weak side behind Vaught. They were beating our brains out–I think the final score was 84-0–and I spent all my time begging Lumpkin to come around our side. He didn't like the insults I added, and believe me, he came our way. This went on for about ten plays and Vaught begged me with tears in his eyes to keep my mouth shut. Vaught was taking out Lumpkin's interference, but that left me to fill the hole and try to tackle this ox. Even with a perfect tackle "Father" would still carry me ten yards.

I could never forget "Father" Lumpkin, who later played in that famous Georgia Tech–California game in the 1929 Rose Bowl. That's the game where Roy Riegels, the California center, grabbed a loose football and ran the wrong way for sixty yards until a teammate, Benny Lom, overhauled him at the three-yard line. Yes, I remember Lumpkin–and I still haven't got around to forgiving Newell, who is an industrialist in Fort Worth and the brother-in-law of Byron Nelson, my old caddying buddy and a Poly graduate who became one of the greatest names in golf.

One afternoon we were playing Decatur High School on the old Decatur Baptist Junior College field. The field had no grass and was full of rocks. Allen Conner, beginning his first season as quarterback, was calling the plays. He called on me to carry the ball four straight plays, and I told him to mix it up a bit. I was the team captain, but Allen called the same play once again. When he did, impulse got the better of me.

I can't explain it, but I stepped out of the huddle, walked around behind Allen and kicked him square in the butt. The Decatur fans laughed their heads off at my silly action. It was certainly out of character for me, but I recall it because impulse would crop up from time to time later in my coaching. I hope Allen, a Fort Worth attorney, forgot all about it years ago.

Discipline, with team togetherness, wins football games, and I owe my grandmother a lot of credit for teaching me the value of both. She was a disciplinarian–and a tremendous influence in my life. She really made me bear down on my school work. She kept a sharp eye on my report cards. Those grades had to be right. I liked to study, though, and I didn't feel I was being abused. I enjoyed it.

In the summer, I mowed the front and back lots, including the one with those chickens. I couldn't get away with a sloppy job of mowing. Grandmother wouldn't tolerate anything that was half done. She would make me mow it again and again to have it right. It also was my chore to go get the groceries on Saturday. And I guess I washed as many dishes as any other boy in Fort Worth between 1925 and 1929.

My last two summers at grandmother's, I went out to Odessa, Texas, and worked as a roughneck in the oil fields. I saved my money and bought my own clothes. I felt a certain self-reliance, and that's a good feeling. It gives you pride. I didn't realize it at the time, but grandmother taught me the qualities of good leadership. She taught me to listen, and to think before I spoke. She couldn't tolerate a phony, and I've never been able to either.

In my senior year at Poly, my classmates elected me president. And, again thanks to grandmother's supervision, my school work was of such quality that I was chosen valedictorian, something Lon Evans and my other classmates will never let me forget.

Valedictorians in those days had to make a major address on graduation day, and I was no exception. I spent a lot of time writing mine out—and memorizing it. Boy, did that teach me a lesson. I was halfway through the speech when I forgot my lines. It embarrassed the hell out of me, and I've never tried to memorize anything since.

Archie Manning brought back memories of my blunder when I went to Washington with him as guests of the Washington Touchdown Club. When they called on Archie to come up and receive the Walter Camp Memorial Trophy he said, "I've been sitting here so long I've just about forgotten my speech."

My Fort Worth buddies kidded me about my memory lapse, but grandmother understood. She never said a word about it. I loved that remarkable woman. I felt, however, that

I had let her down. She taught me that something half done was a failure, and that fits my coaching philosophy.

Coach Francis Schmidt of Texas Christian University in Fort Worth and Coach Matty Bell of Texas A and M at College Station offered me football-work scholarships in 1929. Bell had gone to school at North Side in Fort Worth and was a great coach, but I decided to go with Schmidt. He had swept across Texas like a prairie fire, recruiting football players at a pace never seen before at TCU. I would be in good football company just five miles from grandmother's house on Millett Avenue.

Rube Leissner may have spoiled me a little in my senior year at Poly. I went to Texas Christian University thinking I was going to be a fullback. It was a foolish thought. I'm sure Jackie Simpson and all those other high school fullbacks, including Gene Hickerson, who became guards or tackles at Ole Miss will get a good chuckle out of this. Leo "Dutch" Meyer was the freshman coach under Francis Schmidt in 1929, and my 188 pounds soon found a guard slot.

One afternoon Coach Schmidt called for the freshmen to come over and run some plays against the varsity. I'll never forget that scrimmage. It was stupid of me, but I didn't put on a helmet when I stepped in at right offensive guard. I remember smiling across the line at Mike Brumbelow, captain of the 1929 team that went undefeated. Mike had come to TCU from Jacksboro, Texas, and had developed into a great player. On my first charge, I was lucky enough to move him out. Or unlucky. On the next play I noticed that he had backed off the defensive line a little and dug his feet in. There should have been warning bells in my head.

On the snap, I went after him again. Mike, a natural left-hander, crossfired his best punch to my face. Blood squirted out. After a stunned second, I forgot football. It darn near took the entire team to break up the fight.

I learned two things in my first scrimmage at TCU. First, all football players should wear helmets. Second, I had met a man who would become a lifetime friend—the team captain.

After Brumbelow graduated, I asked for his jersey number—
44. A modest amount of hero worship never hurt anyone.

In those long ago days, Francis Schmidt had to be the most
fantastic coach in the country. He was, at that point—I don't
think there is any doubt about it, it is a matter of record—
way ahead of everybody offensively.

He believed in moving the football and he instilled that
idea in me. Schmidt would do anything to move the ball,
using every kind of offense in the world—including a tremendous amount of ball handling, with triple options and all that
sort of thing.

Texas Christian used an unbalanced line and I was the
strong guard, the middle man in the formation, which meant
that I had to do a lot of pulling. Schmidt ran my legs off. I
pulled on everything that was run on either side, right or left.
Lon Evans, the other guard, pulled a lot too. One day, Lon
pulled left and I pulled right. We hit head-on, darn near kill-
ing ourselves. Now someone busted a signal. I should say it
was Lon, but I won't because I don't want him to arrest me.
Lon is sheriff of Tarrant County these days.

Unlike my uncles, who kidded me about losing to the
Masonic Home's "little bitty orphans," Francis Schmidt
didn't kid. He lived and died for football, cussing all the way.
He studied football twenty-four hours a day, and was a real
taskmaster. To the best of my recollection, he only jumped
on me once. I deserved the tongue lashing. Schmidt had given
us a new play and I had not been paying attention. When he
called out the number I looked at him and asked: "Coach,
where do I go on that?" Schmidt shrieked: "Go to hell!
Maybe they can use you there as you are not doing me any
good!" That's as light as an erring man ever got off the hook
with Francis Schmidt.

In 1964, Jim Browder, then sports editor of the *Fort
Worth Press*, wrote a prize-winning column about Schmidt.
Here are excerpts:

> Francis Schmidt, perhaps the greatest coach the Southwest Con-
> ference ever has known, wouldn't trust his grandmother as far as he
> could throw her.

He could teach new cuss words to a sailor. He lived, breathed, ate, drank and slept football. And, during his five-year stay at TCU, he compiled the greatest football record of any coach in Southwest Conference history—46 victories, six defeats and five ties.

Schmidt trusted no one—doubted everyone. If a football or basketball prospect walked into his office in TCU's little gym during the early thirties, Schmidt would leap to his feet, grip the boy's hand and start pumping. All the time he was engaging in this enthusiastic handshake he was carefully maneuvering the boy backwards to a designated spot on the wall where he had nailed a tape measure. He wasn't shaking hands, he was measuring the prospect to see if he really was as big as he claimed! Then he would feel his muscles and put him on the scales.

That was Francis Schmidt. He was a football genius—100 per cent dedicated to sports—absent-minded—energetic—holder of a law degree—a musician—a terrible driver—and a legendary character of the coaching fraternity. A busted signal on the practice field could cause Schmidt to go berserk. TCU had an off-tackle run—Play 72—that Rex Clark busted one day in scrimmage.

'Damn it!' shouted Schmidt as he began chewing out Clark. 'We'll run that play 72 times if we can't get it right.' Then he made the team run the play 72 times with Clark carrying the ball each time. After practice Schmidt discovered that someone had let the air out of all four tires on his car. Was it Clark?

The most oft-told story concerning Schmidt was an escapade with a grease rack. The man never stopped thinking about football—his mind raced in that direction 24 hours a day. Once he drove into a service station for a grease job. No, he didn't have time to get out of the car, he'd just sit and work on his notes while the attendant greased the car. Up went the rack. The greasing began. Suddenly, Schmidt was brain-struck with an idea. He pushed open the door and stepped out. Ten feet below he wound up as a dusty heap on the ground.

Managers, quarterbacks, photographers and officials caught the major portion of Schmidt's wrath. Once when a decision went against him, Schmidt called for his manager. "Run over to the band, son, and tell 'em to play 'Three Blind Mice' and dedicate it to the officials."

That was Francis Schmidt—the original absent-minded professor.

Just about all of those stories about my college football coach are true. Schmidt coached at Arkansas before he came to TCU, and after the 1933 season he moved on to Ohio State. He built legends everywhere he went. For some reason, he took a liking to me. In those days we had very little film study, but Schmidt managed to get pictures of some of our

games and some of the opposition. I can remember going
with him to the physics lab to review them. It wasn't done by
squad. It was a privilege to be asked to study films with him.
They were dull, dim, no-account films, but I could see their
value immediately. Attention to detail was one of Schmidt's
secrets.

By 1932, the freshmen on the 1929 team had developed
into a championship team, one it was my honor to captain.
No school in the Southwest Conference could stop us. There
are many Texans who say the 1932 team must be ranked
among the all-time squads in the Southwest. This was its
record:

1932

TCU	Opponent
14...North Texas State	2
3...LSU	3
55...Daniel Baker	0
34...Arkansas	12
17...Texas A and M	0
68...Austin College	0
27...Hardin-Simmons	0
14...Texas	0
16...Rice	6
8...SMU	0

It would be useless conjecture to compare our line with
others such as Fordham's "Seven Blocks of Granite" or the
front men on Ole Miss' 1959 "Team of the Decade" in the
Southeastern Conference. But six of our seven linemen were
All-Southwest Conference selections.

I think we would have made a clean sweep, taking seven of
seven, but one of our ends, Dan Salkeld, spent a long time on
the injured list. Teammates—and they were great ones—
making the honor list with me were End, Madison "Pappy"
Pruitt; Tackles, Ben Boswell and Foster Howell; Guard, Lon
Evans and Center, J. W. Townsend. The credit must go to
them; those are the boys who enabled me to make the 1932

All-American team. It was the first time a TCU man had been chosen, but Francis Schmidt had started the ball rolling. Dutch Meyer would keep pace with Sammy Baugh, Davey O'Brien, Charles "Ki" Aldrich, I. B. Hale and others.

In my own case, I owe a lot to my line coach, Ray "Bear" Wolf. He taught me how to block and tackle. Once, in a bull session, Wolf told me that if he ever became a head coach he wanted me to be his line coach. I never thought much more about it.

I suppose everyone who saw the Texas–TCU game in 1932 is waiting for me to mention Harrison Stafford. Well, I didn't dodge him then and I don't plan to now. Through the years the story has become confused and distorted. *Time* magazine in its November 26, 1960, edition, did a story on my Ole Miss team and had this to say about me:

> "Back at Texas Christian they still remember one tackle made in 1932 by All-American guard John Vaught that left both the ball carrier and himself lying senseless on the field."

In a sports symposium in 1970 in Fort Worth, Buster Brannon, the left-handed quarterback on our championship team and now the assistant athletic director at TCU, recalled the Stafford incident this way:

> "I guess the hardest, toughest I ever saw a man hit was when Harrison Stafford of the University of Texas blocked Johnny in an open field block. It *was* the hardest I've ever seen a man hit. They say, and I'm sure it's true, that thereafter Johnny never was quite the football player he was before then. It was a terrific block."

Dutch Meyer took part in that session and he said: "I remember the block. It's nationally known. Johnny got the tar knocked out of him and nobody thought he'd get up, but he did and he went on playing."

At that point Bear Wolf broke in to add: "John took a bead on Stafford the next time around and blocked him pretty good."

What's the truth? I think the *Press* cleared it up in its series on "TCU's Greatest Games." One of those games was our 14-0 triumph over Texas—despite Stafford's block. Here's the published version:

> The play they all remember so well occurred in the third quarter. It was an uneventful period except for Harrison Stafford's brutal block on Johnny Vaught, who is one of the nation's top coaches now at Ole Miss.
>
> This play has become a football legend—one of those that people even today claim they saw when they were no closer to the stadium than a Chinese gunboat.
>
> Some inconceivable tales have been told about it. Everything from Vaught being carried off in a stretcher to the Frog All-America challenging Stafford to a fight after the game. What really happened was this: Bohn Hilliard was returning a Buster Brannon punt in his own end of the field in the third quarter when Stafford bore down on Vaught, first man ahead in the coverage. Stafford took a clear, 10 yard run at Johnny from the blind side in the open field. The Longhorn caught him legitimately (it wasn't a clip) with his flying shoulder—right at the waist.
>
> They say you could hear the impact, and maybe so. At any rate the momentum of the blow knocked Vaught sprawling with such force that his headgear actually was jarred off. Vaught was out for a full minute, and Stafford was somewhat shaken himself. But after the timeout Vaught was back on his feet, strong as ever and uninjured. As mentioned, he played the full 60 minutes. The fact is, Stafford threw another block that day on Pappy Pruitt which sent the TCU wingman out of the game for recovery and left him limping for a week.
>
> Further evidence of the game's rocking quality is this:
>
> Four Longhorns and three Frogs had to be helped off the field. Texas end Sears Earle suffered a broken collar bone, center Bill Smith had a twisted ankle, tackle Herschel Moody went out with a bruised hip, and Hank Clewis left with an injured knee.
>
> Pruitt, Dennis and Dan Salkeld were TCU casualties.

That doesn't leave much for a man to add. But we scored shortly after I got that lick. When we were lining up for the kickoff, I told Evans and the others they should go for the ball. I said I was going for Stafford. A stupid thing to do but I ran right through him on the kickoff. Youth!

Football occupied a lot of my time at TCU, but I never forgot I was there to get an education. I tried to follow my grandmother's advice and study some each day. At first, I thought I wanted to be a geologist, but as the semesters went by my thinking began to change. When I graduated from high school the Graybar Electric Company, an electrical supply firm, gave me a summer job. Its men in Fort Worth urged me to study business and to come back with them after college. This was in the back of my mind when I shifted to physical education and business.

Frankly, I found I didn't have time to take the geology courses. But you must remember this: in 1929 colleges didn't have athletic scholarships as we have today. We had work scholarships at TCU. Every athlete had to put in time to pay for expenses. I had to work three hours a day at campus jobs, doing anything that needed to be done—from carpentry to plumbing. In my senior year, my job was to clean up the music rooms. As I recall, there were several classrooms and a small auditorium. This job didn't take nearly as much time, and I was able to study more and to keep my grades at an honor level.

Until my junior year, my college courting was limited. Then I met Marjorie Scott, a pretty girl from Victoria, Texas. Scottie and I never became engaged, but we had an understanding. Thinking back, I'm sure Scottie must have wondered about my dedication to football. I knew our 1932 team had a good shot at the Southwest Conference title, and I suggested Scottie stay out of school during the fall semester. I didn't want any distractions. Now that's fine for football, but, that's also a good way to drift away from a beautiful friendship.

Francis Schmidt coached basketball as well as football, and each winter after football I turned out as a candidate. Coach Schmidt probably wanted me as a guard on the squad to keep me in shape for football. That was routine forty years ago. But I was too proud to think of such a thing then. I had played basketball at Ingleside and at Fort Worth Poly.

Buster Brannon, Ad Dietzel and the other good basketball players called me the team's "hatchet man," though not to my face. I was a sort of wrecking crew. One night we were playing the Original Celtics in the TCU gym, Joe Lapchick, a six-five center and an all-time pro basketball player, was having a big night. Schmidt sent me in to try to slow him down. Finally, we got into a brawl under the basket, and the officials ejected both of us. The Celtics had lost their star.

After graduation in 1933 I received several job offers and took the post of line coach at North Side High School in Fort Worth. In a year I decided that the work didn't suit me. It wasn't the coaching, it was the teaching. It took a lot of time to prepare lessons. I felt I just wasn't doing an adequate job preparing, that it was unfair to the students. In the meantime, Graybar Electric officials had asked me to come back with them. I decided to do that, and they sent me to Houston in 1934 for their training program. My pay was $125 a month, which was a good sum in those depression years.

While working for Graybar Electric, I bought—and paid for—my first car, a 1934 Chevrolet. Uncle Edell, a retired Government meat inspector who still lives at 3410 Millett Avenue, likes to tell friends I was darn particular about that car, too. Uncle Edell has his reasons.

"Funny thing about Johnny and cars," he once said. "When he lived with us we would let him drive the Model T occasionally and I can remember him coming home one day with the windshield smashed. He said he didn't know how it happened. Later, we had a Model A and Johnny was using it one Saturday to do the grocery shopping. He was driving near Poly and not paying attention when a streetcar caved in the back end.

"But, you know, when Johnny bought his own car he never got a scratch on it!"

I was anxious to progress in the electric company, but I worked as a shipping clerk. I thought I should be doing more. Quite unexpectedly, my telephone rang in the spring of 1936. It was Bear Wolf, calling from Fort Worth. He was keeping a promise he had made years earlier.

"Johnny," he said, "I've been named head coach at the

University of North Carolina. Still want to be my line coach?"

I made up my mind overnight. The money was three times what I was making. I told Bear the next morning I would go to Chapel Hill with him.

I drove my Chevy to Chapel Hill, tailgating Ray and Martha Wolf all the way from Fort Worth. We stopped overnight in Memphis and Ole Miss, 75 miles away, never entered my mind. We arrived in Chapel Hill too late in the spring for the regular drills, but the Southern Conference gave Wolf permission for one extra week just before school let out for the summer.

Chapel Hill is a beautiful town. But it took me awhile to get used to the mountains. It was a different world. I felt hemmed in, but I fought off homesickness with work. Bear and I spent practically the whole summer studying pictures of the 1935 season, trying to learn about the players we had coming back. My time at the University of North Carolina grew into six satisfying seasons. The Tar Heel record under Wolf was 38-17-3, and we won a number of big games in Kenan Stadium, a magnificent playing field set among the legendary Carolina pines.

Like Oxford, Chapel Hill blends cultural and intellectual achievement well with a smalltown atmosphere. There's inspiration in tranquility if a man takes the time to seek it. President James K. Polk was a graduate of the University of North Carolina, and Thomas Wolfe and other literary and academic figures left big footprints on the campus. I felt an academic challenge in Chapel Hill, a need to go back to the books. I recognized some of my deficiencies, and I decided to work on my master's degree.

Off-campus, life was free and easy. I first shared an apartment with Charles P. "Chuck" Erickson and Walter Skidmore. Later, Chuck and I got one together. A great halfback at Carolina under Chuck Collins, Erickson served many years as athletic director. I remember him as an affable and handsome man. Chuck's a grandfather now.

From time to time, I would visit my clan back in Fort Worth. Sometimes, I would go on out to the J. R. Coady Ranch in west Texas to hunt turkeys and ducks with J. R., one of my oldest friends. Fields and streams appeal to my nature, but, in those days, I wasn't entirely a creature of the outdoors. I can't say I was a Fred Astaire, but I liked to dance and go out on the town.

In 1929, when I was a freshman at TCU, I had met a pretty, dark-haired young girl whose Aunt Johnnie happened to be married to my Uncle Lynn. If it was love at first sight we sure missed the signals. Johnsie Stinson's home was in Chattanooga, which is a lot closer to Chapel Hill than Fort Worth, but we never got around to dating until we met again in Fort Worth in 1938.

Those dates changed the game plan. I went back to Carolina a man in love, at the age of twenty-nine. I began writing letters and charting a trip to the Broadway Baptist Church in Fort Worth, where Johnsie and I were married on December 23, 1939. The minister was a young southerner, Dr. Douglas Hudgins. He would be back in Mississippi, at a big church in Jackson, when Johnsie and I reached Oxford.

It didn't take me long to discover that I had married a football fan. Until our son, John, was born in Duke Hospital on June 23, 1942, Johnsie came out to the field and watched our practices. I set up a room in my house for film study with the staff and I remember the night Johnsie tiptoed into the room and asked, "If I stay quiet, can I watch too?" The staff voted her in. Later, she told me she didn't really know what football was all about until she sat in on our film sessions. All my friends tell me she's quite a cheerleader during our games.

In the kitchen, Johnsie quickly learned that I have a peasant's outlook—good food is good to eat. I do have one failing—ice cream. I guess every farm boy who only got ice cream after summer combat with the crank on a hand freezer builds up a reservoir of desire. Johnsie knows how to keep the refrigerator stocked. If I ever get fat, ice cream will be the cause.

Our first apartment in Chapel Hill surveyed the hills from the top of a garage, but we were quite happy there and elated at being a part of Carolina's football world. Wallace Wade, one of the fabulous names in collegiate football, coached Duke, our major rival, in those years. It took some doing to whip that old fox, but the Tar Heels defeated his Blue Devils twice, 14 to 6 in 1937 and 6 to 3 in 1940, while Bear Wolf was head coach.

I've thought of those days hundreds of times. There were many fine football players during my stay at Chapel Hill, including several All-Southern players—Andy Bershak, Jim Hutchins, Hank Bartos, Elmer Wrenn, Crowell Little, Steve Maronic, George Stirnweiss, Paul Severin, Bill Faircloth and Jim LaLanne.

Those were good years, but by 1939 there was war in Europe and Asia. I was aware of the world situation but the Japanese attack on Hawaii on December 7, 1941, came as a stunning surprise.

3

The Cloudbusters

Patriotic fervor swept through all of us on the coaching staff at Carolina after Pearl Harbor and we volunteered immediately for Navy duty. I was the first to be accepted and the Navy sent me to Annapolis for six weeks of training that would earn me my V-5 lapel pin that I treasure to this day.

At Annapolis I met a remarkable figure in the history of collegiate football, Tom Hamilton, then a lieutenant commander. Under his leadership in December, 1941, the Navy Pre-Flight and Physical Training Section—the V-5 program—became a reality in colleges and universities. It was a stroke of luck for me to be in the first indoctrination class and to hear Hamilton say, "There are certain qualities desirable in an aviator which can be developed through the medium of football."

Then he added: "In varsity sports the competitive spirit is developed to the highest degree."

When the Football Writers Association of America met at Des Moines, Iowa, on December 12, 1942, it chose Hamilton as football's Man of the Year, a tribute for his decision to use college football to help train Navy fliers. I agreed with the selection, but it wasn't until the war was over that I realized the value of the V-5 program to the coaching profession. Credit must go to Hamilton, a Navy hero as a football player and as a fighter at sea. Between 1923 and 1926 Hamilton, now a retired Admiral and executive director of the Pacific-8 Conference, won nine letters at the Naval Academy. When his organizational work was completed and the pre-flight program was underway, Hamilton went back to sea as executive officer of the carrier Enterprise.

Modern football owes much of its popularity explosion to Hamilton and the men who became Cloudbusters and Seahawks. His idea created a cross-pollination of coaching skills unlike anything the country had ever seen. Day after day at the pre-flight schools—Georgia, North Carolina, Iowa, California, St. Mary's and many more—coaches from each great section of the nation worked together and picked each other's minds. Techniques and ideas learned in the V-5 program would bear fruit in peacetime at Ole Miss and other schools.

During the war Hamilton's brilliant plan played a tremendous role in helping to keep college football alive. At one time or another more than 300 colleges gave up the game. There were some critics of Navy policy—the Army did not have a similar program—but on December 3, 1943, a reporter for the Associated Press asked Secretary of the Navy Frank Knox if he was satisfied with regulations which permitted cadets to play football during pre-flight and other college training programs, such as V-12.

"Very much so," he replied.

Later, a spokesman for the Department of Navy said: "We put on a big scale football program mainly because we believe the sport is an important phase of combat training, and, in doing so, we probably saved college football from oblivion."

Among the first V-5 coaches were Bernie Bierman, James Crowley, Harvey Harmon, Paul Bryant, Ray Wolf, Harold Drew, Gomer Jones and such distinguished Mississippians as

Tad Smith, Buster Poole and Parker Hall. Other great coaches and players quickly joined the group. By August 9, 1943, when Don Faurot, the father of the Split-T at Missouri, replaced Bierman as coach of the Iowa Seahawks, some of the brightest young talent in the country had assembled at Iowa City. Faurot's assistants included Larry "Moon" Mullins, a former Notre Dame star; Elmer W. Holm, former line coach at Nebraska; Lloyd Peterson, one-time Minnesota fullback; James Tatum, former North Carolina coach; Tom Reardon, former Notre Dame and Green Bay Packer halfback; Doug Kerr, Iowa State line coach; and Charles "Bud" Wilkinson, former quarterback and assistant coach at Minnesota. Out of that brain trust would come the coaches who turned Oklahoma and Maryland into national powerhouses.

There was a similar marshalling of coaches at other Navy Pre-Flight schools. When my training ended at Annapolis I was assigned to the North Carolina Pre-Flight program for 1942, and I worked as an assistant to James "Sleepy Jim" Crowley, former Fordham coach and one of the Four Horsemen on Notre Dame's fabulous 1924 team. Crowley used Knute Rockne's Notre Dame system in 1942, and we had a lot of good football with our Carolina Cloudbusters.

A storyteller of first rank, Sleepy Jim—I never called him that to his face—kept us laughing with his wit. The story he most liked to tell involved a conversation with Coach Rockne at Notre Dame. Rockne, who once said Crowley always looked like he was just falling in or falling out of bed, called Sleepy Jim aside one day at South Bend and asked him: "Is there anything dumber than a dumb Irishman?" Crowley said he replied: "A smart Swede!"

The Navy reassigned me to the prep flight program at Rensselaer Polytechnic Institute in Troy, New York, in 1943. There, the Navy trained men just entering service, and I was in charge of cadets and set up the program. I didn't do any coaching that season. Every month several hundred new men would arrive in Troy, and I worked as hard as I ever have just to keep up. One day a slim little man walked up to me and volunteered to help me—without pay. He was Doc Knight, the athletic trainer at Rensselaer. I never forgot his help and in 1947 I called on him to help me once again—at Ole Miss.

In 1944 the Navy promoted me to lieutenant commander and transferred me to the Corpus Christi Naval Air Station in Texas and put me in charge of the physical training program. Once again the V-5 program and a Notre Dame man would play a role in shaping my football thinking. This time it was Moon Mullins, who had been with Faurot at Iowa Pre-Flight. I was surprised when Mullins told me he had shifted away from the Notre Dame box. It was not that he loved Irish football any less, but at Iowa he had discovered he loved the Split-T more. Day after day Moon would tell me the Split-T was the greatest thing he had ever seen. The formation got its name from splits in the offensive line, and Moon swore a coach didn't have to have super-athletes to make the Split-T go.

After duty hours I would sit with Mullins, Tilden "Happy" Campbell and other coaches to discuss football. There was no way for me to know that a football idea born at Missouri, brought to maturity at Iowa Pre-Flight and scattered across the country by Navy coaches would one day help Ole Miss football.

When the war ended all of us were anxious to get back on the job at some college. Early in 1946 Campbell approached me about joining an old Alabama friend, Harold "Red" Drew, at the University of Mississippi. I had to look Oxford up on a map, but one of the big attractions in joining Drew was his Navy background. I told Campbell I would think about it.

4

Oxford

In the big band days of the 1930's and the 1940's the Peabody Hotel in Memphis symbolized the Deep South. Writers considered it a landmark. Both David Cohn and William Faulkner said that the Mississippi Delta began in the lobby of the Peabody. There's a lot of truth in that, as many Ole Miss supporters know. I guess there are more Mississippians in Memphis, Tennessee, than in any other city in the world.

A lot of people remember the Peabody for its ducks in the lobby fountain. At exactly five in the afternoon the darn things waddle over to an elevator and go up to the Penthouse. That's funny to watch, but the Peabody sticks in my mind for another reason. I checked into the hotel in mid-February of 1946. With the war over, ex-Navy officers who had been college football coaches scattered across the country like birdshot. When I got out of the Navy at Corpus Christi on February 2, I was uncertain about the future. Technically, I suppose, I could have gone back to the University of North Carolina. But I had not heard from anyone there, and I have

never asked for a job in my life. I took my wife and young
son up to Fort Worth from Corpus and visited my parents.
Much of my time there was spent thinking about three job
offers.

A few days later I drove to Memphis. My mind wasn't
made up, but I was headed for Oxford to talk to Red Drew,
who wanted me to sign on as his line coach. That night at the
Peabody I thought about the other offers. Ray Wolf, the
head coach at North Carolina when I was an assistant, had
moved on to the University of Florida. Bryan Brannon, a
teammate of mine at TCU, and Paul Severin, a fine player at
Carolina, were going to Gainesville to join him. I was tempted
to fall in line. Bear Wolf and his wife, Martha, were close friends
of mine. The other offer had come from Moon Mullins, who
took the head job at St. Mary's after leaving the Navy. I ran the
possibilities through my mind until I fell asleep.

My family had stayed in Fort Worth, so I got up early the
next morning. My road map to Oxford had been marked with
a red pencil. As I stepped out of my room and turned to
close the door, I got a hell of a shock. Someone had drawn a
cartoon character on my door. It stared me right in the
eyeballs. Under the chalk drawing the artist had written:

SCHMO WAS HERE

I still wonder who did that. I hadn't heard any noise
during the night. I'm not superstitious, but I wonder if it was
some kind of omen. That damn Schmo stuck in my mind as I
took Highway 51-South out of Memphis into Mississippi. To
get to Oxford from Memphis, you go six towns south and
turn left. I remember Hernando, Coldwater, Senatobia,
Como, Sardis and Batesville. About 20 miles east of Batesville
I topped a ridge and in the distance on another ridge I could
see a row of brick buildings, starting with the military science
hall on the west. Nowadays, the Ole Miss skyline includes the
silvery dome of a coliseum, but not then.

I drove my little Olds coupe onto the campus and began

looking around. My first impression was one of utter dismay. Although it had only about 2,000 students, Ole Miss seemed crowded. Many war veterans were back on campus, and flight jackets and olive drab clothing could be seen everywhere. I stayed in the Student Union and I saw cigarette butts all over the place. I guess I still had the mentality of a Navy lieutenant commander serving as the duty officer. I thought the Student Union was the dirtiest place I had ever seen.

Coach Drew welcomed me aboard. So did Happy Campbell, who had urged me at Corpus Christi to join Drew. Ole Miss offered a coaching challenge. I knew the school had never been able to do much in the Southeastern Conference, but I decided to become a Rebel. I figured if the staff went all out to get good players that had been going to Coach Allyn McKeen down at Mississippi State we would do all right. I had had this State boy—Harper Davis—down at Corpus in the Navy, and I knew Ole Miss could win with its share of Mississippi boys like him.

Later, I learned that Drew and Campbell, who had been assistants at Alabama, had their hearts set on returning there when the chance arose. I certainly can't fault them for that. Under Coach Frank Thomas, those Red Elephants, led by a skinny passer named Harry Gilmer, had bounced Southern Cal in the 1946 Rose Bowl. When you think of Alabama, you think of great football traditions. My own situation differed from that of Drew and Campbell. I was a Texan in the wilderness and my intention was to help Drew build a winner at Ole Miss.

It appeared to me that would take time. Frankly, I had a hard time adjusting to conditions at Ole Miss. The athletic facilities in 1946 were pitiful. The athletic office—one room—was in an old gym. Assistant coaches had to stand around or sit on the steps. We often sat in cars for our football staff meetings.

When I had time I would drive into Oxford, which adjoins the campus. Nestled in the hills of the Pontotoc Ridge, a last little toe of the Appalachians, Oxford is steeped in tradition and, for the most part, proud of the fact. A Confederate soldier stands stiffly at attention on his tall stone pedestal in front of the courthouse square, gazing down Lamar Street. Lucius Quintus Cincinnatus Lamar was a distinguished Mississippian who served as a United States representative, a senator, Secretary of the Interior in President Cleveland's cabinet and associate justice of the United States Supreme Court. Lamar's statesmanship won him a chapter in President John F. Kennedy's book, *Profiles in Courage.*

Oxford also was the home of Nobel Prize-winning novelist William Faulkner, who saw a game only now and then but never held the sport against us. Over the years we built up a nodding acquaintance. By coincidence, Faulkner wrote *Sartoris, The Sound and The Fury, As I Lay Dying, Sanctuary* and *Light in August* between 1929 and 1932—my football years at TCU.

Under Ed Walker and Harry Mehre, Ole Miss football had experienced some successes, but not everyone took an interest in it. To a coach, Saturday is a different day, a world all its own. But in 1946 Saturday was also a big day for the farmers who lived in rural Lafayette County. Oxford is the county seat and the university had to face the fact that a lot of the farmers didn't know or care that 15,000 people were yelling their lungs out a mile away from the square. I suppose many of those who heard the cheers wondered "what in tarnation" was going on. But times change. Today, they and their children are sitting in the stands at kickoff time.

It would be wrong if I leave the impression that Oxford is just like Jefferson, Faulkner's Yoknapatawpha County town. It isn't. It may have been ideal for film settings of the Old South at one time, but that's in the past. If a visitor gets caught on the inside lane down at the square on Saturday and tries to work his way out he'll understand traffic jams.

Oxford was incorporated by legislative act in 1837, but it is older than that, having been a trading post in Chickasaw Indian country. It took its name from the great English university because the townfolk hoped the Mississippi legislature would put the state university in Oxford. When possible sites were narrowed to Oxford in the hills and Biloxi on the Gulf Coast, a committee inspected both sites. According to one historian, "One look at the mosquitoes and water moccasins around Biloxi drove the site to Oxford."

Classes began at Ole Miss one crisp November morning in 1848 with 80 southern gentlemen enrolled. One published report said the students brought slaves as attendants, together with hunting dogs and guns. George Frederick Holmes, the first president, welcomed them but had no idea what he was getting into. The Reverend John N. Wadell, a faculty member who later became chancellor, said: "No more crude and disorderly set of young men ever assembled in any college." Little more than a year later President Holmes left the campus to regain his health.

But the scions of Mississippi's planter aristocracy settled down gradually, and one of the greatest figures in American education, Frederick A. P. Barnard, served as president and chancellor of the University of Mississippi from 1856 to 1861. Barnard, later president of Columbia University in New York, expanded facilities rapidly. It was under his guidance that the largest telescope in the world at that time was ordered in Europe for Ole Miss. But the Civil War broke out and the telescope went to Northwestern University. It has been written that Dr. Barnard took over at two "second rate" institutions—Ole Miss and Columbia—and turned them into outstanding universities.

A sense of history is a necessity in Oxford. A stranger has a lot of catching up to do in Mississippi, a fact that forced me to read anything about the state that I could get my hands on back in 1946.

I fell in love with the autumn weather. By October, it is so refreshing in our hills that you wake up willing to pay for such beautiful days. It must have been that way in 1893, the year football began at Ole Miss. On November 11, Dr. A. L. Bondurant, a Latin professor, collected a sufficient number of students and defeated a visiting South West Baptist University team from Jackson, Tennessee, 56 to 0. The players were early risers in those days, often beginning their training at 5 o'clock in the morning.

It was a pleasant surprise to read that two great eastern universities gave us our team colors. In 1893 Dr. Bondurant put it down this way:

> The team had much discussion as to the colors that should be adopted, but it was finally suggested by the manager that the union of the Crimson of Harvard and the Navy Blue of Yale would be very harmonious, and that it was well to have the spirit of both these good colleges.

Time has not changed the colors or diminished the spirit. That comes home to me when I think of Glenn Cannon, an All-American safety on the 1969 team, who said: "When I have to take off that blue helmet with the red stripe for the last time I just don't know how I will do it."

Harvard's link to Ole Miss' school colors rings a bell with me. In 1929 *The Parrot*, my high school annual at Fort Worth Polytechnic, predicted I would become football coach at Harvard. But the road led to Oxford, not Cambridge. Ole Miss, that's my home. I learned quickly in Oxford that Ole Miss isn't a nickname for the university. It's a synonym that goes back to 1896 when Miss Elma Meek of Oxford suggested that the yearbook be called Ole Miss, a term family servants used in antebellum days in talking to the plantation owner's wife. A daughter would be addressed as Young Miss.

A contest to pick an athletic nickname was held in 1936 by *The Mississippian*, the student newspaper. Two hundred suggestions surfaced and Southern sportswriters, serving as judges, picked Rebels, an entry submitted by Judge Ben Guider of Vicksburg.

In the 1930's one student, Bill Richardson, son of the state's champion whittler, showed up to claim his football scholarship with two bird dogs and one suitcase. In 1946 there was nothing like that, but I'll never forget one morning in my first spring at Ole Miss. I heard a noise and I walked outside the gym to see if my ears were deceiving me. They were not for there's no clickety-clack so distinctive as a farm mowing machine. A man everyone called Big John sat on the mower, but it wasn't pulled by a tractor. I remember shaking my head and saying:

"Good God amighty. Mules!"

5

Win The Big Ones

It was a game with Arkansas in 1946 that opened my eyes to the value of winning the big games, the ones the fans remember. Orville Henry of the *Arkansas Gazette* in Little Rock took note of my attitude about this in a column in 1970 and suggested that my Achilles heel revealed itself in losses to teams Ole Miss should have whipped easily. He may have a point, but let's return to 1946 and look at the events that shaped my thinking.

The year was a hectic one. Like homing pigeons, coaches flocked to old and new roosts from military duty. Many of them showed up on campus wagging a ball player or two behind them. That practice has just about died out, but I was guilty of it in 1946. I brought a Texas boy, Ray Bornemann, to Ole Miss with me. Coach Drew dragged in one or two from Great Lakes Navy, so you can see the picture. The day of practically all our players coming from Mississippi had not arrived. One of our better players was Bill Erickson, who lived in Bayside, New York.

We had an abundance of football candidates at Ole Miss but a scarcity of good athletes in shape to play. There were some young kids, but many of the boys had been in military service and had wives. That great World War II social contribution to America's campuses—Vet Village—blossomed at Ole Miss as well as at other colleges. Bornemann happened to be among the married and the University of Texas and his wife wanted him in Austin. I think I have learned how to handle players, but I confess failure in knowing how to deal with their wives.

Ole Miss lost Bornemann. Just after the Christmas break, Bornemann loaded up his convertible and a big, fat chum of his from Texas, Jim Cullen, whom the other players dubbed "Ray's valet." Then Bornemann went up to the room of the team manager, J. A. "Bubba" Blackwell, about midnight and knocked on his door.

"Bubba," he said, "I'm leaving. Coach Vaught and them don't know it. Goodbye."

I found out about it the next morning. Ray was a fine athlete. He later helped Texas win a trip to the Orange Bowl. But all was not lost. I learned something too—the value of getting athletes close to home and single.

In fairness to Coach Drew I think a brief explanation about the 1946 season is in order. Ole Miss lost seven of nine games, but only Mississippi State, which had Tom "Shorty" McWilliams, Harper Davis and Billy "Spook" Murphy in its backfield, beat us as much as 20 points. All of us worked hard but too many of our players tried to run on sea legs. As Buddy Bowen once said, "Charley Conerly was just back from the Marines and wasn't in shape, and I was in worse shape. I had been sitting on a parachute for four years."

There were other factors, too. When Drew took over from Harry Mehre, the situation at Ole Miss was not ideal. There was a strong pro-Mehre faction on the campus, including a number of ball players who had signed a petition requesting that his contract be renewed. As I mentioned earlier the athletic facilities were in sad shape. C. M. "Tad" Smith, one of the great men in Ole Miss athletic history, had returned from the Navy and taken over as athletic director. Tad would shoulder the burden and start us on the road upward, but little could be done overnight.

At the start of the season Ole Miss didn't have complete uniforms. We had to borrow red jerseys from the University of Alabama for our first two games. A few of the older boys resented this and one or two of them spoke bitterly of the team as "the little Crimson Tide." Ray Poole, the team captain, was not among the grumblers. "We were lucky to get the jerseys from Alabama." he said. "Ours had been ordered but everything was difficult to get the first year after the war."

The fact remained that Ole Miss didn't have complete uniforms and Alabama had enough to lend. I think that makes a good point about our plight.

Ole Miss lost its opening game in 1946 at Lexington, Kentucky, and the difference was Ermal Allen, who ran for one touchdown and passed for another to give Coach Paul "Bear" Bryant's team a 20 to 6 edge. The mention of Allen, now an assistant coach with the Dallas Cowboys, brings up a curious incident in Southeastern Conference history. A week before the season opened, the SEC schools by an 8 to 4 vote ruled that Allen was ineligible, contending that the 5-10, 160-pound halfback had already played three years of varsity football before the war. But, on Friday before the Ole Miss game, the conference's executive committee, overrode that decision by a questionable 2 to 1 vote. On Monday, the executive committee's last-minute action was thrown out by the conference presidents.

Strangely, in ruling that Allen had played out his eligibility in 1939, 1940 and 1941, the conference let the score stand. Ole Miss still held the short stick. Mrs. Drew, who had known Bear Bryant since his playing days at Alabama—Red Drew had been the end coach there—didn't like all this. Her son, Pinky Drew, told a close friend that she saw Bryant after the game and said, "Paul, don't ever set your foot in my house again for what you have done to my family." The

Southeastern Conference, begun in 1933, had its problems
with such issues. But, in 1946, it was beginning to come of
age. It had a commissioner even then. His office would increase steadily in prestige in the future, but Walter Stewart, a
great boxing and football writer for the *World-Telegram* in
New York and *The Commercial Appeal* in Memphis, wrote:

"Mike Conner is paid to run the football affairs of the
Southeastern Conference, and we believe that he is thor-
oughly capable of running it, but he has less freedom than
the guests of Alcatraz."

Conner, a former governor of Mississippi, pioneered the
way for us as commissioner. He was followed by Bernie
Moore, who ably served the SEC for many years, and A. M.
"Tonto" Coleman, the present commissioner. Conference
headquarters are in Birmingham. Final authority rests with
the university presidents, but the commissioner today has
great responsibility involving our athletic programs. In the
SEC with Ole Miss are Mississippi State, Louisiana State, Alabama, Auburn, Tennessee, Kentucky, Vanderbilt, Georgia,
and Florida. Onetime members, Georgia Tech and Tulane
now play as independents.

Ole Miss worked hard at winning in 1946, but couldn't
quite cut it. Coach Bobby Dodd of Georgia Tech told his
boys that Mississippi "pushed harder and moved less than any
other team in the conference." Perhaps he was right. But
there was a major upset in the making for Ole Miss' non-
movers in 1946. It came October 26 in Memphis against
Arkansas of the Southwest Conference. Ole Miss whipped the
Razorbacks, 9 to 7, and never did a big win come at a better
time. The week before, Ole Miss had embarrassed itself and
the conference by losing to little Louisiana Tech, 7 to 6, at
Oxford. Happily, I didn't have to see it.

Coach Drew had assigned me to scout Arkansas. As it
turned out, the trip to Austin for the Arkansas-Texas game
would prove influential in my selection as head coach at Ole
Miss the following year. Now I don't believe in super-
stition, but a funny thing happened when I went to Austin.

On my way down I called an old roommate of mine at TCU, Ad Dietzel, and asked him to join me in scouting Arkansas. I flew to Houston and drove to Austin, where I met Ad. As we were walking into the stadium I happened to look down and noticed a green wad of paper along the sidewalk. I picked it up and unrolled it. It was a dollar bill.

"Ad," I said, "this is a good omen. You sign this thing right now." I was being facetious about it being an omen.

As for the game, the United Press wrapped it up nicely in its first paragraph:

> AUSTIN, Texas, Oct. 19.—Arkansas put up a defense Saturday that stopped the Texas Longhorns like a four-strand barbed wire fence, but it had no barricade for the brilliant passing of Bobby Layne, whose tosses accounted for all the touchdowns in a 20 to 0 victory.

After the game Ad and I went back to our hotel room to write up the scouting report. We got through about 9:30 that night and went out to eat. As we walked up to the door of a restaurant I looked down and damn if it hadn't happened again. There lay another dollar bill. Ad signed that one too.

To upset Arkansas, Ole Miss decided to use a gambling six man front—something that I had picked up from Sleepy Jim Crowley at North Carolina Pre-Flight in 1942. Against Arkansas we moved the line around a good bit, overshifting and undershifting to stop the running of Smackover Scott, who had returned from the United States Naval Academy, and Ross Pritchard.

Arkansas scored first on a pass from Kenny Holland to Alton Baldwin, an end, in the third quarter. Then a bit of irony went to work for us. Ray Poole, an end who played 56 minutes of the game, came out for a breather. During that brief interval his replacement, Everette "Hairline" Harper, tackled Howard Hughes, a Porker tailback, behind his own goal to give us two points. With two minutes and 50 seconds remaining, Charley Conerly, whose passing had amazed 25,000 fans all afternoon, found the same Mr. Harper open behind the tense Arkansas secondary. Charley whipped the ball toward him. The throw was short, but Hairline lived up to his name. He caught the ball at his shoetops and tumbled happily on his head in the end zone as Arkansas' Scott and Leon Campbell looked on helplessly.

It should be noted that Coach Drew made an inspiring talk to the boys before the game. It was rather personal. Actually, Red had come to Ole Miss on the rebound. Before he signed at Ole Miss, Drew thought the Arkansas job was his. But at the last minute John Barnhill of Tennessee got it. Drew's speech had impact with the boys, but he publicly gave me a lot of credit for the victory in interviews with reporters. It was a nice gesture, but I worried about it because other members of the staff worked just as hard as I did.

Drew's statement about my role got around among the alumni. That always comes back to help you.

You never know why you keep certain mementos, but I still have those dollar bills I found and Ad Dietzel signed in Austin when we were scouting Arkansas. So there it is: find dollar bills and win the big ones.

6 Johnny Vaught Named Ole Miss Head Coach To Succeed Drew

A Major Decision

Rumors of Coach Drew leaving Ole Miss to return to Alabama were in the newspapers on January 13, 1947, but I knew nothing official until later in the day when Drew told me he had resigned to go to Tuscaloosa, where he had served 11 years as an assistant to Frank Thomas. Illness had forced Thomas to step down. Red asked me to go with him and I was tempted. My thoughts centered on Alabama's great traditions and fine football.

I suppose the hours between Drew's offer and my decision to stay at Ole Miss were the most fateful in my career. There was speculation in the newspapers that I was in line for head coach, but I wasn't sure I wanted the job.

After 10 years on a pretty safe raft as an assistant, I felt I was ready to step up—that was my ambition—but I wanted to be sure I could build a winner at Ole Miss. Between 1893 and 1946 there had been 26 coaches at the University of Mississippi, and only Ed Walker, one of Pop Warner's stars at Stanford, and Harry Mehre of Notre Dame had lasted as long as eight years. As for winning in the tough Southeastern Conference, the best Ole Miss had been able to do since 1933 was to win three conference games in a season. Not without reason, many observers thought Ole Miss was too small and isolated to do much.

But events have a way of sweeping you up and controlling your destiny. In the athletic dormitory, the boys made an expression in my favor. Conerly, Bowen, Poole and others got to influential alumni, including Tommy Turner of Belzoni, Britt Rogers of Tupelo, Martin Van Buren Miller of Meridian and Lake Roberson Sr. of Clarksdale, and asked them to support me. Fortunately, these men were already talking to me about taking the job. To be truthful, there was one drawback in going to Alabama. I figured I would have to take a second row as a coach. Hank Crisp was the line coach under Thomas and everyone knew he would stay under Drew. That was the picture when Tad Smith, the athletic director at Ole Miss, called me into his office.

"John," Smith asked in that pleasant drawl of his, "are you ambitious?"

"I certainly am," I said.

Looking back, it seems foolish of me, but I didn't take the job then and there. I talked to Miller and other alumni. They convinced me they would band together and help me break the lock Mississippi State seemed to have on much of the football talent in our state. Also, I wanted to talk to one of my oldest friends, Mike Brumbelow. A great player and assistant coach at TCU, Mike had spent part of the 1946 season as a scout for Ole Miss at my suggestion. There was no money in the athletic budget for such a post, but the Loyalty Club, an incorporated alumni group headed by Turner, paid his salary.

Mike ran a sporting goods store in Midland, Texas, and I put in a telephone call to him. With the aid of the chief of police out there, I finally tracked Bumbelow down.

"Mike," I said, "I can go to Alabama with Coach Drew or stay here at Ole Miss as head coach for about the same salary. What do you think?" He didn't hesitate. "Hell, Johnny, take the head coach job. You can get fired at Ole Miss and still go to Alabama or most anywhere as an assistant."

Then I revealed the real reason I had made the call. I was worrying about assistants. I told Mike that some of the best football players ever produced at Ole Miss were available, but none of them had much coaching age on them.

"Mike," I said, "I'll tell you what I will do. I will take the job as head coach if you will come down for the football season to give us more experience on the staff."

Brumbelow, who had been Dutch Meyer's asssistant at TCU in the Davey O'Brien days, replied: "No, Johnny, I can't leave my business." With that, I became a salesman. I lit into a series of promises. I think I overloaded myself, but I promised Mike a good salary and expenses; Ole Miss would buy 50 pairs of football shoes from his store; Ole Miss would buy 50 pairs of shoulder pads; and Tad Smith would pay cash.

The telephone remained silent. In desperation I added one more promise. "I guarantee you, Mike, if you will come on down we will throw the Yo-Yo pass you wanted to use against Tennessee last year at least six times against them this season."

Mike's voice cracked back from Texas: "When do you want me to report?"

The Yo-Yo did it. Mike and I dreamed up the Yo-Yo pass for the Tennessee game in 1946, but Ole Miss never used it. Coach Robert Neyland's defensive ends at Tennessee had a definite style of play. If you ran at them they would come up. If you passed, they would drop back. Mike and I figured that by a little fakery we could work them like a Yo-Yo.

Later, Mike, a great storyteller, said, "Well, John, you may as well know the truth. It wasn't just the Yo-Yo promise that brought me back to Ole Miss. Every man has his price and you passed mine with the shoe order."

When our telephone conversation ended, I went to Smith and told him I wanted to be the football coach at Ole Miss. We shook hands. It was Tuesday, January 14, 1947. Outside, the Alabama-bound coaches were waiting for me in their car.

They kept honking the horn and yelling, "Come on, Johnny!" I finally went out and told them goodbye, that I was staying. My pay was $12,000 a year, a good salary then. I got a big chuckle in 1946 when reporters asked Jess Neely of Rice if there were any truth to the report that Frank Howard of Clemson had been offered $10,000 to be his assistant. Coach Neely replied: "If there's a $10,000-a-year assistant's job open, tell them I am an applicant."

Reporters came to see me the day I took the Ole Miss job and I held my first interview as a head coach. It probably wasn't the wisest thing to say, but looking at the published accounts I discover that I said: "The general standard of football players at Ole Miss is not quite up to that of other colleges and I recognize this as our biggest problem. We're going to start tackling it on February 3 when we start spring practice."

In a separate interview, Charley Conerly said, "If the football team had had a choice it would have been Vaught. He's a fine fellow on and off the field." Now Mr. Conerly, a junior in 1946, had caught my eye too. We would see a lot more of each other, including one rather widely discussed head-to-head confrontation about Charley's off-the-field proclivities.

My first night as head coach I went to the athletic dormitory to talk to the boys. I got there about 8:30 and we had quite a session. They promised to play their best for me. When I finally got home my wife, Johnsie, and I discussed my decision. I don't know if every man does the same thing, but I wondered if I was ready for the challenge ahead. I would be matching wits with some of the great names in college coaching—Bobby Dodd at Georgia Tech, Paul Bryant at Kentucky, Red Drew at Alabama, Carl Voyles at Auburn, Bernie Moore at Louisiana State, Allyn McKeen at Mississippi State, Ray Wolf at Florida, Red Sanders at Vanderbilt, Henry Frnka at Tulane, Wallace Butts at Georgia and Robert Neyland at Tennessee.

I certainly wanted to be ready to coach in such select company. I was 37 and I knew I had to make good quickly. When sleep came I was thinking about organizing my staff. In that regard, fate smiled for me.

7

"A Walking
Hall of Fame"

While I was an assistant at Chapel Hill, I heard a lot about Thomas Wolfe, the big, talented novelist who attended the University of North Carolina and later wrote *You Can't Go Home Again.* Until I reached Ole Miss, I felt there was a lot of truth about not being able to go home again. But that theme doesn't seem to apply to Mississippians. They are strong believers in family and state ties. I think they are like their own literary genius, William Faulkner, who never really left Oxford.

Mississippians have a feeling for Ole Miss and their state that's difficult to define. But it's real; it exists. Ole Miss' football players remain a part of the family long after graduation. The door remains open at all times. The truth is that my coaching assistants simply came home.

To add coaching age to my staff, I pleaded with Mike Brumbelow to leave his store in Texas and join me as a part-time assistant in 1947. Since then, we've done our own aging. Only two fulltime assistants left Ole Miss during my 24 seasons as head coach. That's remarkable staff stability, and it's got to be one of the secrets in our success.

The day I became head coach, James E. "Buster" Poole happened to be visiting the campus, and I hired him on the spot. A distinguished member of a remarkable family of athletes, Buster started as end coach and moved up to defensive line coach when the staff was reassigned in 1951. A big friendly man who could get down in the trenches with the boys, Buster was an All-Pro player with the New York Giants in 1939-40-46. He put the first polish on his coaching skills in the Navy V-5 program.

My offensive line was coached by Frank "Bruiser" Kinard, who is an immortal in Ole Miss athletic history. In 1948 Bruiser led the voting of the Christy Walsh board in selection of All-American tackles for the modern era. In his 1936 season at Ole Miss Bruiser played 708 of a possible 720 minutes. A charter member of the Football Hall of Fame, Bruiser was a pro star with Brooklyn and New York between 1938 and 1946. In 1945, while in the Navy, Kinard captained the Fleet City team in San Francisco that featured the running of Buddy Young of Illinois. One of four brothers to play at Ole Miss, Bruiser came home in 1948.

It was no accident that the senior members of my staff were Navy men. All of them had been exposed to different coaching ideas. That's one reason I went down to Southwest Louisiana Institute at Lafayette in 1947 and hired Johnny Cain, my offensive backfield coach. Cain, who played under Wallace Wade and Frank Thomas at Alabama and was an All-American, served as a lieutenant commander in the Navy. John A. Hovious, an Ole Miss star who was half of the famed "H-H" tandem with Chief Hapes in the Harry Mehre era, coached my defensive backs. Hovious returned to Oxford at the request of Red Drew in 1946 after serving as a Navy lieutenant, and I asked him to stay with me.

Roland Dale, captain of my 1949 team, now coaches defensive lines and linebackers. He's a cousin of our Navy clique, having served in the Marine Corps in 1946-47. Roland was with the Washington Redskins in 1950, but turned to high school and college coaching after a shoulder injury. He came home in 1960.

Ole Miss' field representative is Thomas K. Swayze, who is as shrewd as an oldtime horse trader. Swayze joined me as a fulltime recruiter—the first in the Southeastern Conference— in 1947. Tom, also an excellent baseball coach, can see the potential in a boy better than any other coach I know.

An ex-Marine and one of Buster's younger brothers, Ray Poole handles field goal kickers and works with the "B" team defensive line. My freshman coach and varsity scout was Eddie Crawford, a Rebel halfback who graduated in 1957 and played pro football with the Giants. Billy Mustin works as a "B" team offensive coach and resident manager of Miller Hall, the athletic dormitory. He was a fine little halfback and a great punt returner before his graduation in 1950. In 1968, I added Bob Tyler, a young man who never played college football but attended Ole Miss and became a successful high school coach, to work with wide receivers.

When baseball permits, Jake Gibbs works with our quarterbacks. Jake, a catcher with the New York Yankees, also helps in scouting and recruiting. It's the trainer who keeps a football team going, and Doc Knight has been the indispensable man in our program since 1947. A graduate of Springfield College, Doc is a converted Yankee from Providence, Rhode Island. As I mentioned earlier, he earned his V-5 button with me at Troy during World War II. I also must mention Billy "Nub" Sanders, a 1952 graduate of Ole Miss and our efficient equipment manager since then.

In an article published December 21, 1969, Orville Henry, sports editor of the *Arkansas Gazette,* said this after visiting our athletic offices:

"A fan can walk in after lunch any middling day and hobnob with Buster or Ray Poole, or Bruiser Kinard, or Junie Hovious, or Jake Gibbs, or any others in this living, walking, talking Mississippi Hall of Fame who make up Vaught's staff." Indeed. The names of assistant coaches at Ole Miss are household words in our state. In Southaven, a new town just across the state line from Memphis, streets have been named for the coaching staff. Half of a head coach's battle is won if he gets good assistants and keeps a happy atmosphere. Everyone on the Ole Miss staff knows what he has to do. It is much easier to coach when you have assistants who can work in specified areas, yet see the same overall picture that you do.

My assistants spoke up at staff meetings. I didn't want a bunch of yes men working with me. I like coaches who are their own men, and that's what I had. Once, in a newspaper interview, Kinard said: "Coach Vaught leaves a lot of the work to the individual coaches. He'll throw something out and let us fit our pieces to the puzzle. That certainly is to my liking. If the head coach won't let you help, it hurts." Bruiser said something else that struck me: "I always go to work with the feeling that no one on the staff will ever leave Ole Miss."

We were all very close—like one big family—and my assistants worked hard to produce winners. The challenge is too great at Ole Miss for anyone to become complacent. Many times the senior members of the staff were approached about head coaching jobs elsewhere, but they stayed in Oxford. There's something about Ole Miss that gets next to you, and it means more than money. The main thing was that we got along.

Years ago, the University of Houston was soliciting an Ole Miss prospect in Mississippi, and I thought the recruiting was a little stronghanded. I called the Houston athletic director and complained. To be truthful, I didn't get much satisfaction from him. My staff heard me end the telephone conversation with these words: "Okay, okay, if that is the way you feel about it, but there goes our fine relationship." Occasionally, those words came back to me. When I spoke too sharply to an assistant he could slow me down by saying, "Okay, okay, if that is the way you feel about it, but there goes our fine relationship." Well, it was that kind of association from the beginning—1947 and Ole Miss' first conference championship.

8

Conerly To Poole

I don't deny beginners luck in 1947. After all, only Ole Miss had Charley Conerly and Barney Poole, a passing combination that did as much as anything I know to kill the old Seven Diamond defense. Completing 133 passes, Conerly broke "Bud" Schwenk's 1941 national record. Poole, a big end who could turn his back on a defender and catch the ball as well as any man I ever saw, pulled in 52 passes, also a national record.

When I shook Tad Smith's hand and accepted the head coach's job, all thoughts that Ole Miss was a coaching graveyard had been put out of my mind. Otherwise, I would have jumped into that car carrying my friends to the University of Alabama. Yet, it never dawned on me that Ole Miss could turn 1946's disappointing 2-7 around in just one year.

The same bunch of boys produced these contrasting results:

	1946		**1947**
	(2-7)		**(8-2)**
Ole Miss 6	Kentucky 20	Ole Miss 14	Kentucky 7
Ole Miss 13	Florida 7	Ole Miss 14	Florida 6
Ole Miss 0	Vanderbilt 7	Ole Miss 33	South Carolina 0
Ole Miss 7	Georgia Tech 24	Ole Miss 6	Vanderbilt 10
Ole Miss 6	Louisiana Tech 7	Ole Miss 27	Tulane 14
Ole Miss 9	Arkansas 7	Ole Miss 14	Arkansas 19
Ole Miss 21	LSU 37	Ole Miss 20	LSU 18
Ole Miss 14	Tennessee 18	Ole Miss 43	Tennessee 13
Ole Miss 0	Miss. State 20	Ole Miss 52	Chattanooga 0
		Ole Miss 33	Miss. State 14

When spring drills began February 3, 1947, I kept an eye on Charles A. Conerly of Clarksdale. During the 1946 season I had decided here was an athlete who could make or break a team. Charley had told me that he wanted a career in pro ball, and he appeared to have the ability. A war veteran who had been a freshman on Harry Mehre's talented 1941 squad, Conerly had the markings of a super-athlete. He could throw the ball, and that was what I was interested in doing. In those days, Charley's teammates called him "Roach," a nickname he picked up playing baseball with the Clarksdale Roaches in the Mississippi Delta.

I felt in 1946 that Conerly just wasn't in good enough shape to play 60 minutes of football. In the spring of 1947 I sensed that he was still up to his old habits. An ex-Marine, Charley had had a rifle shot out of his hands by a Japanese sniper, and, like a lot of boys who had fought in the Pacific and won, Conerly liked to live it up a bit. But I decided it had to stop. I called Charley in for a talk with me and Tad

Smith. In our 45-minute session I did most of the talking. You could never tell what Charley was thinking by looking at his face, as college and pro defenders would discover. But he sat there and listened to me—with the silent, alert look of a falcon. I spoke bluntly:

"Ole Miss is going to throw the ball this fall, Charley, and you will have every opportunity to exploit your passing abilities. But I'm expecting more out of you than you have shown. You have got to stay out of honky-tonks, get yourself in shape and dedicate yourself to a fine senior year."

Somehow my words hit Charley. He agreed with me. Later hitching at his trousers, Conerly stood before his teammates and said:

"I have done everything there is to be done, that can be done, but I'm dedicating myself to football this year. If I can do it, the rest of you can. Let's get together and do something."

That must have been one of the longest speeches Conerly ever made—about 37 painful words. And Charles didn't lie. He curtailed his off-the-field activities. I think he knew that I met with the team before I met with him and told the players we planned to win with him or without him. Charley and I have hit it off ever since that session. Long before fall practice began in 1947, Charley called Farley Salmon, a halfback who also lived in Clarksdale, and said, "Fish, let's get started early at home." The captain of the 1947 Ole Miss team was ready to play on September 1.

In the spring we didn't know we would have our famous Conerly to Poole battery, a pair of touchdown producers who have to rank with Howell and Hutson at Alabama and O'Brien to Looney at Texas Christian.

Poole, an All-American end for Coach Earl "Red" Blaik at the United States Military Academy at West Point, had told his family and friends that he wanted to leave Army and return to Ole Miss, where he had been a freshman with Conerly. To put it mildly, we wanted Barney. Ole Miss needed him to replace his brother, Ray, who had graduated after the 1946 season. And Ole Miss got Barney.

A lot of stories—many of them highly colored—have been told about Poole's return, which came a year after such athletes as Shorty McWilliams of Mississippi State, Clydell "Smackover" Scott of Arkansas and Bob "Hunchy" Hoernschmeyer of Indiana had left the military academies.

Ole Miss did not kidnap Poole from West Point. I don't think you can deal with the military that way. Barney came to Ole Miss of his own accord, although a two-man delegation did make a wild, funny trip to see him. The famous safari got started when Smith, our athletic director, and Tommy Turner of Belzoni, a planter who has helped us through the years, got to talking about Poole at the National Collegiate Athletic Association meeting in New York in 1947. They knew Barney had been trying to resign.

"Tad," Turner said one afternoon, "why don't we go up to West Point and tell Barney to come on down to Ole Miss?"

Smith liked the idea. He suggested they hire a limousine and go up the Hudson in search of Barney.

"I know the military mind," said Smith, who had been a Navy officer. "We'll get up there just before dark and when they see you and me sitting in a limousine, Tommy, they'll wave us right through the gate."

Smith was right. But once inside, they didn't have the slightest idea of where to go. Cadets weren't allowed to use a telephone unless summoned by the duty officer. Smith and Turner didn't want to arouse suspicion anyway, so they started driving around the academy grounds. It was a classic case of a blind hog finding an acorn. Pure country luck took Smith and Turner to Poole, who recalled the incident this way:

> Glenn Davis and I were coming out of the gym where we had been practicing basketball when I saw the limousine with Tad and Tommy. If I had come out a minute later I would have missed them. I went over to the limousine and got in—against the rules—and I told them how badly I wanted to come home. There have been stories that I sat on the floorboard of the limousine, but I don't remember doing that.
>
> I told them I had been trying to resign ever since the war ended, but each time I sent in a resignation it came back marked 'Refused.'

Somehow Shorty McWilliams, who wanted to return to Mississippi
State, got his resignation accepted in 1946 in time to play that
season.

Coach Blaik, a fine man, told me it wouldn't look good to flunk
out, but that was the only way. I didn't leave with Tad and Tommy.
I busted a leadership course or two. Even then, they wouldn't let me
go until June. I had to sit and watch my class graduate, and that gets
next to you.

Early in June, Barney came to see me and said he had
enrolled for the summer term. In my first season I would
have two super-athletes in Conerly and Poole. Other things
were happening too.

By adding some offices and a film room to the old gym-
nasium, Smith and I put a stop to staff meetings in cars. And
Ole Miss stepped up its recruiting. My friends who had encouraged me to stay kept their promises. Everyone—coaches
and alumni—put their knuckles to use, knocking on doors at
schools and homes that had been neglected far too long by
Ole Miss. My own schedule was crowded. I spoke anywhere
in the state I could, sometimes to as few as six alumni. In the
process I became a naturalized Mississippian. I quit eating
beef barbecue, an old Texas habit, and switched to pork
barbecue, an old Mississippi habit. I even learned that Mississippians don't pronounce the second "i" in Mississippi.

Neither do I. They know how to welcome a man in
"Mis-sippy." Total strangers would shake my hand and say,
"Come on in, Coach. Make yourself at home. How's your
lovely wife?" That old southern expression, "Kissin' don't
last, cookin' do," must have originated in Mississippi. If finer
tables are set somewhere else, I don't want to go there in
search of athletes. The boys will be too fat.

A major victory for the Ole Miss athletic program came on
March 8, 1947—the date we hired our pipeline to talent, Tom
Swayze. I had only seen him once before, back in the spring
of 1946 when I had driven to Moss Point with Coach Drew
for a high school banquet. Tom was the coach there. When I
talked about hiring a fulltime contact man or recruiter after I

became head coach, Tad Smith and Martin Miller brought up Swayze's name. Finally, I invited Tom to the campus. To show you how shrewd he is: Swayze arrived for the interview with two players—Ken Farragut and Harry Davis. They were the first of hundreds that he would round up for us.

I'm a cautious man myself, and I was pleased that Tom didn't buy my idea with a snap of his fingers. I had to do some selling.

"Tom," I said, "I have to have immediate help and you are the man."

Swayze said the idea of becoming one of the first fulltime recruiters in college football was all right, but then he added: "If I take the job I'll give you two or three years as a recruiter, but when there's an opening on the staff I want to get back into coaching."

We made a deal. Once, perhaps twice, I have had to tell Tom, who also coaches the Rebel baseball team, that I simply can't replace him in our football organization, which is the truth. Nowadays, Tom wouldn't want to change. Under Swayze, a Mississippian who grew up in Raymondville, Texas, then returned to attend Ole Miss, we launched our successful Mississippi-boys-first program. In a later chapter, I'll explain some of our secrets in recruiting, a few of which were picked up by professional teams.

Your first season as a head coach is a little like your first courtship. You never quite get over it. How could I ever forget 1947? I remember it all. It is unlikely that any other first-year coach had so many unusual things happen to him or his team. Some of the events border on the fantastic.

My first team, built around a squad which had gone 2-7 the previous season, received a bowl bid in June—three months before the first game!

Charley Conerly threw 30 passes in his first game, out-dueling Kentucky's George Blanda.

Y. A. Tittle of LSU lost his britches against us, and Conerly, the passer, ran for three touchdowns as the Rebels upset the Tigers, 20 to 18.

And, to the delight of Mike Brumbelow, we used the Yo-Yo pass—and all other kinds—against Tennessee. Ole Miss won, 43 to 13, the worst defeat ever handed a team coached by General Robert Neyland.

It gives me a lift just to think about 1947. Those fellows from Memphis who had come to us in June and offered us $25,000 to be the host team in the first Delta Bowl must have figured they were the smartest, or luckiest, people in the world. A team picked to finish last, or next to last, in the SEC would bring a conference championship to Crump Stadium on January 1, 1948, to play TCU. I don't want to overplay my first season, but I think you'll get an understanding of our football program by looking at some of the highlights, including our opening game with Kentucky on September 20. What a beginning.

It fell my lot to make my debut against Bear Bryant. He rates at the top of my list of friends and coaching adversaries and he brought a good Kentucky team to Oxford for my baptismal. Fortunately, we had just about as close a bunch as we ever had, and we had good preparation before the game. Just before kickoff, a grand old man, Martin Miller, who had been team manager at Ole Miss in 1908, came into our locker room and made an impassioned speech to the boys.

Once Ole Miss took to the field, Conerly was in command, completing 15 of his 30 passes. Blanda, later to prove one of the iron men of professional football, had a bad day, completing 3 of 9. Poole caught 7 passes for 71 yards, and football fans everywhere talked of Ole Miss' 14 to 7 upset—and of Conerly and Poole. But, that day, I think our linemen really made the difference. They forced five Kentucky fumbles and we covered four of them. And Kentucky had fine athletes. In addition to Blanda, the Wildcats had Wallace "Wah Wah" Jones, Jay Rhodemyere, Dopey Phelps, Lou Serini and Harry Ulinski. My starters were Poole, Bill Erickson, Bernie Blackwell, Dave Bridgers, Jimmy Crawford, George Lambert, Everette Harper, Buddy Bowen, Jerry Tiblier, Red Jenkins and Conerly.

Conerly certainly earned his wings that day. He opened the
game by going upstairs, and with just 4 minutes and 59
seconds gone in the first quarter, he stuck one in Poole's
hands for a touchdown. It was the first polish on their fabulous reputation. When I think back, the victory over Kentucky was just about the biggest thrill I ever had in winning
football games.

It couldn't happen today because of a rules change, but
one of our two losses in 1947 was to Coach Red Sanders'
Vanderbilt Commodores, 10 to 6, in Nashville. Late in the
game, Conerly hit Poole with a hard, short pass and the ball
bounced off Barney. Another Rebel 15 yards farther downfield, Joe Johnston, caught it and scored. The field judge just
stood there, moving his feet but going nowhere. Finally, E.
D. "Red" Cavette, the referee, ran up to him, discussed the
play and made the official drop the flag. The play was called
back. In those days if two receivers touched the ball without
a defender putting his hands on it the ball was dead. Red
called it correctly and I didn't make any protest.

But a lot of Ole Miss people, including Martin Miller, who
was listening to the game on radio down in Meridian, didn't
know about the rule. Cavette had hardly reached his hotel
room when the phone rang. It was Martin, calling from
Mississippi.

"How long has that rule been in the book?" Martin asked.

Red replied, "About 25 years."

"Well," Martin came back, "what did Vaught say about it?"

"I passed by Vaught on the sidelines on my way to the
dressing room," Cavette said, "and he didn't say a word."

"If Vaught hasn't said anything," Martin concluded,
"don't read that telegram I just sent you."

Five minutes later the telephone rang again. It was a
woman calling from the Western Union office in Nashville.
She said, "I have a telegram for you, Mr. Cavette."

"Can you read it to me, please?"

"I'm sorry, sir, but I don't read these kind of words over
the telephone."

Cavette, remembering Martin Miller's warning on the telephone, told me he didn't go down and pick up the telegram. He had an idea what it said.

Even in defeat, Conerly looked great. He was a battler. Just to watch him pass was a coach's delight. Our second loss in 1947 came in the Arkansas game. The contest took place in the mud in Memphis, but it was one of the greatest struggles ever put on by two athletes—Conerly and Scott, the old Navy hero who had returned to his Arkansas homestead.

Walter Stewart captured the flavor of the game in this masterpiece in *The Commercial Appeal* on Sunday, October 26:

> Clyde Scott weighs 164 pounds molded upon a framework which is buggy-whip in its clean vibrancy. Charley Conerly carries 19 more pounds into the fury off tackle—is lean and swift and tougher than a cypress knee. They are boys you'd pass on the street without pausing to look back—unless you note a certain falcon intensity in eyes well back beneath level brows.

> Yet, on yesterday's gloom-hooded afternoon they locked in a duel which will be remembered until men speak no more of gallant deeds—will live in little pockets of luminosity glowing down in the black years.

> A long time ago, there was a poet named Homer and he wrote of Achilles' epic wrath—of the god-like courage which was Hector's. But if that blind sagaman could have looked down from Saturday's press box, we believe that he would have added a footnote to the Iliad.

> According to regulations which have worn well, there are 11 men on each football team, but yesterday there were 20, who formed a valiant background as Scott and Conerly spawned their glory in the mud.

> For these were not gods. They were quite mortal boys, each of whom fumbled off a touchdown. They were boys who got tired and wet—whose ankles twisted in the mud. But in the final summing up, their valor and skill-at-arms fit the pattern hewn into a plain which rocked beneath the walls of Troy.

> With a wet ball forced upon him—a ball which squirmed between his hands like a thing alive—Conerly passed 23 times and winged home 14 for 138 yards. He threw for both Ole Miss touchdowns and held

a slashing Razorback at bay with the cunning of his toe. His matchless tackle stopped the first Crimson assault—cut it down with only empty yards behind him.

His cleats slashing madly at turf which would not hold, Clyde Scott ran 20 times from scrimmage and carried forward across 92 bitterly contested yards. He took one of Conerly's towering kicks on the Arkansas 15 and cut through an endless vista of thrashing arms for 61 yards—a rush which set up the second Arkansas score. With the Razorback reeling back and chopping bloody foam from its tusks, Clyde Scott threw a 40-yard pass to the Ole Miss 25—ripped a crater at tackle an instant later and was driven wide at the two. And that was triumph delayed. For Stacey Looney cleared the line with a deer-hound leap and Arkansas had won, 19 to 14.

It was a struggle which shuttled from goal to goal with such maddening speed that 27,950 in attendance scorned dribbling clouds and huddled down for the last tight-bitten minute. In losing this game, Charley Conerly lost none of his All-America stature—rather added to it. And Scott went along hand-in-hand.

You may see a game in which two finer backs are pitted, but we greatly fear that you'll be forced to wait for Valhalla.

Johnny Lujack played for Notre Dame in 1947, but the Southeastern Conference had the greatest collection of passers in football. In addition to Conerly, there were Harry Gilmer at Alabama, Blanda at Kentucky, Johnny Rauch at Georgia and Y. A. Tittle at LSU. Those thrilling LSU-Ole Miss games about Halloween time each year began in 1947.

It was Conerly against Tittle. And, as the sportswriters like to say, the ushers didn't carry out the heart failures—just stood on them in order to see more closely. The score was 20 to 18, Ole Miss, but the event everyone remembers is Tittle intercepting a Conerly pass and running until his britches fell to his knees.

Actually, this was the game Ole Miss had to win to take the championship, and LSU was favored. In the final analysis, Bobby Oswalt won the game for us by kicking two out of three extra points. LSU's Holly Heard missed all three of his attempts, and that was the difference.

After searching the records at Ole Miss and at LSU, I think certain points can be cleared up about the Tittle episode. In his book, *I Pass!*, written when he was with the New York Giants, Tittle said he intercepted a pass in the second quarter and was headed for a touchdown when his fallen britches stopped him about our 20-yard line. He also wrote that Conerly was on the bench at the time.

This book has revealed to me how tricky your memory can be. Often, the record simply says you are wrong. I have had to rewrite many sentences because of that. A portion of the second quarter play-by-play of the LSU-Ole Miss game is interesting. Sent to me by Bud Montet of the Baton Rouge *Morning Advocate*, it reads:

> Ole Miss first down on the Ole Miss 26. Conerly faked a reverse and hit the center for eight yards. Salmon struck through left tackle for a first down on the Rebel 44. Jenkins was smothered on an attempted sweep around left end by Wimberly.
>
> Conerly looked for a receiver, didn't find one, and hit center for a yard to the 42.
>
> Conerly pass was intercepted by Tittle on the LSU 17 and Tittle, holding up his pants with one hand, ran back to the LSU 38.
>
> Time was called for LSU while repairs were made on Tittle's pants.

In addition to sending me the LSU play-by-play, Montet added: "From our observation Tittle never would have scored on the play, broken belt or not."

I think Montet is right. Tittle wasn't the world's fastest human. But he could throw the football.

That pants incident was one of the funniest things that ever happened on a football field. On the interception, an Ole Miss player, possibly Jack Odom, broke Tittle's belt buckle when he tried to tackle him around the LSU 20-yard line. When he came to the bench, Farley Salmon, a defensive half-back, said, "When Tittle's britches fell I couldn't keep from laughing.' Tittle said, 'Dammit, quit laughing and help me get my pants up.' "

Aside from the falling britches, the game was a battle between two of the greatest passers in football history.

Conerly completed 12 of 19 and Tittle hit on 7 of 20. LSU, under Bernie Moore, used a conventional T-formation. Ole Miss ran the Notre Dame box, but we had developed a little criss-cross that always left Conerly at tailback. It was a device that utilized his talents better, and it paid off throughout the season.

In the LSU game, Conerly ran for all three of our touchdowns. Charley never ran much—except for his life in his early years with the New York Giants—but he was a triple threat at Ole Miss, passing, running and kicking. There aren't many like Conerly in the history of college football.

Our last game in 1947 played a tremendous role in our goal to wrest football supremacy in Mississippi away from Mississippi State. Mike Brumbelow had been scouting Coach Allyn McKeen's Bulldogs all year, and, in doing so, had spotted a weakness in their kickoff coverage. Coming downfield, State's right end hugged the sidelines. The man next to him always veered toward the center of the field. So, on the opening kick, Will Glover nearly went all the way by shooting into that gap. Ole Miss was off and running. Again, Conerly had a big day. When it was all over, we had won, 33 to 14. There is no way to estimate how much that victory helped us in recruiting that year, but it gave Ole Miss a tremendous wedge to use. Another big factor was the signing of Conerly to one of the first $100,000 pro football contracts.

Folks everywhere talked about it. Ambitious young Mississippi athletes who wanted to walk in Conerly's footsteps thought of Ole Miss. A detour sign had been put on the old road to Starkville.

The victory over Tennessee in 1947 brought about as much satisfaction as a man can expect as a football coach. Never—never had Ole Miss defeated Tennessee before that game in Memphis on November 8. But all afternoon the stadium announcer kept repeating:

"Conerly to Poole." "Conerly to Poole."

In bright sunshine, Conerly threw four touchdown passes and ran for two more. Three minutes and fifteen seconds after the game started Conerly plunged over from the two for our first score, and after Bobby Oswalt added the extra point there was no heading of Ole Miss. Matching the offense, the defense limited Tennessee to a net of nine yards rushing. After the game, General Neyland, the great Tennessee coach who did not deal easily in superlatives, said, "Conerly is the greatest back I've ever seen."

Walter Stewart wrote:

> And again it was Charles Conerly—it was the Rebel Roach who loosed the storm and ruled the bull-thrusting waves. It was the Rebel Roach who rode the sweeping winds with 19 pass completions and 239 yards—hit friendly hands for four touchdowns and fleshed his fabulous cleats in scoring terrain for two more. It was a ruthless chess he played—it was a one-man show, but it was being played by one of the great football technicians of all time.
>
> If the Roach isn't All-American, neither is Douglas MacArthur.
>
> Another who tied thick knots in the All-America skein was Barney Poole—the big Barnabus who blocked two Tennessee kicks and made a six-point catch just as the ball reached end-zone sod.

These words about the men who made Ole Miss' 43-13 victory possible were written by a man who loved Tennessee football, a writer who had served as a colonel under Neyland in the China-Burma-India theater during World War II. But Stewart, a graduate of Illinois and a player under Bob Zuppke, warmed to the genius of great athletes—and Conerly and Poole were that.

Hearing of Ole Miss' victory over Tennessee, Coach Drew of Alabama sent me this telegram: "Congratulations on the greatest achievement since the invention of the forward pass!"

9

We Swim With

A Fish

Some observers expected Ole Miss to go back to sleep in 1948. It had had its dream year. On the surface, the disturbing thing about my second season was that Conerly was playing with the New York Giants, not Ole Miss. Barney Poole, however, returned for his eighth season—seventh as a varsity player—of college football. In those days, time spent in military service didn't count, even if you played with the University of North Carolina and Army, as Poole had as a Marine in the V-12 program and as a Cadet. I'll admit Ole Miss had an experienced end.

But we were lightweights in most other departments. It was this situation that made me decide to switch to the Split-T. Ole Miss did not have a great passer in 1948, and the Split-T gives you a general, all-around offense with average athletes, as Don Faurot had revealed at Missouri and Iowa Pre-Flight. Moon Mullins had convinced me at Corpus Christi Navy, and I was itching to try it.

In the spring of 1948, Farley Salmon told me he planned

to graduate, although he had a year of eligibility left. A gutty little halfback, Salmon said he wanted to go out a winner, and he had been a right half on our 1947 championship team. When I mentioned our plans to shift to the Split-T his eyes lighted up a bit. He told me he had spent a month practicing as a Straight-T quarterback under Mehre before going into military service.

"I'll stay, coach," Salmon said. We would swim with a Fish.

Fish couldn't pass, but he had quick reactions. He could slide down the line and option the football or throw a little dinky pass. The Split-T in 1948 did not include the 45-degree rollout we use today. But, as it turned out, the Split-T set our section of the country on its ear. People couldn't believe their eyes as Fish, who was about 5-9 and never weighed more than 152 pounds, faked, pitched, ran and passed.

I was as surprised at our success as anyone.

Now, 23 years later, my assistants will be happy to learn that I had doubts, too, about our 1948 venture. I remember their moans about our material, complaining about skinny-legged tackles, slow ends and a quarterback who had to stand on tiptoe to see over the line. I was worried but the staff got to poor-mouthing so bad about the material that I got angry. One day I blew up:

> Listen, the boys are the best we have. They are the only ones we are going to have this season. If you guys are going to coach at Ole Miss this year, you have got to quit griping and start coaching these boys. We have got to join our kids and try to help them win some games. I am damned tired of listening to this crap. Now I'm going to make a telephone call and when I get back I want to start work.

That was a little trick I used from time to time in meetings. I went after a cup of coffee. When I returned the conference room was quiet. Finally, Junie Hovious, an assistant who had never been very critical of the boys, spoke out in a loud voice:

"Coach, while you were gone we all got to talking and, you

know, we have decided that we have a damned fine looking football squad. All they need is a little coaching."

What could I do? I laughed. But from that day on the staff worked hard, and with enthusiasm. And Fish Salmon and his teammates went out and bettered our 1947 season, winning eight and losing only one. That season taught me a lesson— never underestimate a team. Our 6-1 mark in the conference gave us second place. Georgia was first at 6-0.

We started by whipping Florida, 14 to 0, Kentucky, 20 to 7 and Vanderbilt, 20 to 7. In the Kentucky game our defensive backs put on the show of their lives. Billy Mustin, Jerry Tiblier and Dixie Howell piled up 152 yards on three punt returns, Tiblier scoring on a 68-yard run. In his book *Building a Championship Football Team,* Coach Bryant said Ole Miss' success bothered him so much that he abandoned the tight punt formation for a spread that A. C. "Scrappy" Moore of Chattanooga suggested to him.

Tulane whipped us, 20 to 7, in New Orleans, but our team snapped back in Memphis the next week, rolling over Boston College, 32 to 13. Two days before our sixth game—LSU in Baton Rouge on October 30—I walked into my office and found a note from my secretary. It said: "Mr. Dottley wants to see the coach and the quarterback."

I sent a runner for Salmon. When he came in I handed him the note and asked, "What's this all about?"

He shook his head. A few minutes later the door swung open and in marched William Dottley with his son, John "Kayo" Dottley, our sophomore fullback, in tow. The senior Dottley is a little man, but he had his big son by the arm, maneuvering him as a tug does an ocean liner. I managed to say, "Hello, Mr. Dottley."

He didn't answer. He just turned to Kayo and said: "You are dragging your ass. Get up and get going, boy, or come home."

Without another word, the father turned and walked out of my office. I think Kayo's great rushing career at Ole Miss— and later with the Chicago Bears— began right there. In the second quarter against LSU, I sent Kayo into the game. Salmon figured he would be in the right frame of mind, so he called it off tackle for Dottley. Kayo ran over five men—a couple of them were ours—going in for the score. It was a big night for Ole Miss. With seven different men scoring, we trounced LSU, 49 to 19.

The 1948 team also defeated Chattanooga, 34-7, Tennessee, 16-13, and Mississippi State, 34-7. State, our major rival for Mississippi talent, was in trouble. Allyn McKeen left after the 1948 season, and a parade of coaches put State's program in a wobbly condition. Swayze told me that everywhere he went in 1948 high school athletes liked the way the Split-T moved the ball. The recruiting tables had turned.

Fish and his teammates would have made a good showing in a bowl. The Cotton Bowl gave us one nervous look, but its officials probably thought Ole Miss had stumbled into two fluke seasons in a row. Our football reputation still had to be established.

10

Platoons Anchor Us

It hurts, even after 20 years of healing, to talk about 1949 and 1950. But they are in the records. They aren't going to go away. So the time has come to face up to the facts—to discuss platoon football, a $3,000 fine levied against Ole Miss and Ronald "Rocky" Byrd's shoes.

Excellent material, dedication and fair coaching are the things that have made Ole Miss a winner in football. You don't win games with gimmicks. I think Rocky's shoes tell a lot about my two worst seasons—years that left Ole Miss with a dismal 9-10-1 mark and the extreme discomfort of growing pains. Byrd, our quarterback, was about 5-10, and it was felt that he needed an extra inch or two to see over the linemen so he could pass better. To build him up, we put cork in his shoes.

Our troubles went much deeper than elevator shoes. Ole Miss simply was not ready for platoon football when it burst on the college scene in 1949. The era of one or two super-stars pulling a team out of a hole was over. Kayo Dottley, who had been up and running ever since his father dragged him into my office and chewed him out, was the leading rusher and scorer in the SEC that fall, but his 1,312 yards and 84 points couldn't bail us out. It takes 44 pretty good boys to play the game with unlimited substitution, and Ole Miss could not meet such a manpower demand then.

Looking back on those dismal times, I'm not sure I was ready for this new approach. Platoon football calls for specialists—one-way athletes. Everything in my background had been built around the best athlete—a boy who played offense and defense. It seemed in 1949 that the one big puzzle the staff and I had been working to put together suddenly became two.

Those years depressed me. It was the only time I seriously considered leaving Ole Miss. I don't like to lose, and I told myself that if I couldn't win I wasn't going to stay in the game. I would do something else.

Fortunately, none of us on the staff afforded ourselves the luxury of crying. It struck me that if I left Ole Miss and took another job I would be walking away from a job undone— something that would have put a frown on my grandmother's face. And mine.

I would have been a quitter. I decided to work a little harder. I thought about 1948 and Hovious' remark that all the boys needed was some coaching.

The low point in our program came on October 1, 1949, when Kentucky and Babe Parilli, a sophomore quarterback, made amends for the two upsets Ole Miss had sprung on Kentucky in 1947 and 1948. They buried us, 47 to 0. But I had been forewarned. On the Monday before the game, Brumbelow came back from scouting the LSU-Kentucky game and said, "Johnny, I have just seen the greatest quarter-back since Davey O'Brien." Mike was talking about Parilli.

Ole Miss had whipped Memphis State and Auburn by iden-tical 40 to 7 scores going into the Kentucky game, but the Wildcats ran us off our own field. A bit of historic irony, perhaps, but Doug Hamley, a tackle who had captained our 1948 team, was ruled ineligible the week of the game on a complaint by Kentucky that he had played three varsity seasons. Ermal Allen, you'll remember, had been knocked off the Kentucky team for the same reason in 1946. The action upset the team, but it was the game that upset me.

Some of the players complained that our playbook must have fallen into Kentucky's hands or there had been a spy in the camp. When our quarterback called an audible, such as "Red," a Kentucky defender would look at the end involved and say, "I've got you covered, Red." I'm skeptical about that. Perhaps the "Red" incident was one of those strange coincidences. All I want to say is that Kentucky had done a good job scouting us. Frankly, the big trouble was with our boys. I didn't think we were getting everything out of the boys, and we had a pretty stern meeting where I told them so. That's the only game Ole Miss ever played under me that I didn't show the boys the game film. Maybe my action was selfish; perhaps I didn't want to relive a nightmare. But I felt there wasn't anything on the film that would do Ole Miss any good.

Marriages hurt us as much as platoon football in those days. Just before the 1969 season I saw that the marriage situation at Ole Miss once again was getting out of hand. I put out a policy memo that had to be signed by each married player. I wish I had put that memo out 22 years ago in 1949—when Vet Village was in full flower. It said:

The University of Mississippi
Department of Intercollegiate Athletics
University, Mississippi
September 15, 1969

A problem has been created by matrimony, and it is imperative that we have a complete understanding. Naturally, my concern is for our football squad and having and maintaining the greatest morale and esprit de corps possible.

All of you know that it has been my policy and belief that marriage and football, on a college level, do not mix well. To be a good football player and to be a good team man, it is necessary to sacrifice many social pleasures. In marriage, an individual takes on many obligations and added responsibilities. Therefore, the attention given to football suffers.

I feel sure that some of you will not play up to your potential, and I am forced, therefore, to assume the attitude that you will have to "show me" before I can put implicit confidence in you. Football is at least second, and maybe further down the line, in your interests.

I am willing to give you some special privileges. In return, I expect, and must have, complete cooperation and no deviation from the regulations. You will live in the dormitory Wednesday through the game day. When the game is away from the campus, you will stay with the team and return with the team. Once back on the campus, you may have your home privileges through Tuesday of the following week.

I want you to study the above. Any deviation from this policy will subject you to removal from the squad. If you are in accord with the above, sign this letter and return it to me. If you are not in accord, turn in your uniform.

                                        John H. Vaught
                                        Head Football Coach

If this book reveals anything, it should let you know that I am not against motherhood. Football has been a family affair at Ole Miss, but there is the matter of timing.

Back in 1949-50, Ole Miss players were having children by platoons, and I think that definitely was a factor during our two worst seasons. To be successful in athletics you have to have togetherness, and I felt we weren't getting the team togetherness that was necessary. Marriage, to me, takes an awful lot away from boys in college. It's an institution in itself. Living successfully married is a big job, and it takes time from football. In other words, a boy comes to Ole Miss to get an education and when he has the added responsibility of maintaining a happy home something has to give if he is an athlete. I thought football was giving. I could see clearly that marriage and parenthood were distracting the team.

Ken Farragut, a fine football player and captain of our 1950 team, and his wife became the parents of a girl in January. "My first one was a girl," he told his teammates, "but I'll tell you one thing, the next one is going to be a boy." That suited me fine. But when the boy came in December of the same year of the girl I decided to talk to Ken. I remember calling him in and asking him if he knew where the babies were coming from. He said he did. I didn't kick him in the butt, as I did Allen Conner back at Fort Worth Poly, but I was rather impulsive. I reached into my pocket, pulled out a half-dollar and pitched it on the table. "Ken," I said, "that will solve your problem." Eighteen years later, Ken, who played pro football with Philadelphia, brought a son and daughter down to Ole Miss and enrolled them. They are fine children. But I wish he had waited awhile.

After the 1950 season I decided it would be in the best interest of Ole Miss football to offer scholarships only to unmarried athletes. It's a little bit ridiculous to think anyone can go to college on a Southeastern Conference scholarship and maintain a family. Some help has got to come from some place. Either the family has to provide it or somebody has to work. But it has been our experience at Ole Miss that the wives can't work for long because they have babies—despite the pill.

I admit that our marriage rules have been bent from time to time, but we stuck to the principle as best we could. The situation changes a little if a boy gets married after he starts his college work. But a flexible "no marriage" rule helped to put Ole Miss on the road to better football.

Naturally, the rule cost us a few good athletes. Lance Alworth, the great flanker for San Diego, is a good example. Lance wanted to come to Ole Miss, and we finally signed him at Brookhaven High School. In the meantime, he got married. Ole Miss still would have taken him, but, due to the job situation at Ole Miss and other complications, Lance ended up at Arkansas where he had a distinguished career as a half-back. I saw Lance at the Washington Touchdown Club in January of 1970, and we got to talking about old times. He agreed with me that it is much better for an athlete to play in his own state. That surprised—and pleased—me. It's been my theme all along.

Ole Miss took a painful kick from the conference in 1950. In the first week of June that year, I set up a coaching clinic and invited Bud Wilkinson to lecture to about 250 high school coaches. Bud's Oklahoma teams used the Split-T that we used.

Wilkinson held a four-hour session of lectures and demonstrations. Conerly and Ray Poole, both then with the New York Giants, aided in the demonstrations, as did Dixie Howell, who had been a fine halfback for Ole Miss in 1947 and 1948.

I made the mistake of using two squads of my own players to run plays at the clinic. This had been done at numerous coaching clinics, including the one Frank Leahy of Notre Dame conducted for us a year earlier. There was nothing to hide. Our sports publicity department sent out a news release saying Coach Wilkinson had praised our quarterback, Rocky Byrd, who took part in the demonstrations.

Something else brewed trouble for us, too. Coach Neyland at Tennessee got his dander up when Ole Miss signed five prep stars out of Memphis—Jimmy Cole, Joe Gaynor, Hugh Ballard, Ronnie Case and Billy Russell. Frankly, Swayze had skimmed the cream. Somehow, Neyland considered Memphis exclusive University of Tennessee territory, although it is almost 400 miles from the University of Tennessee and only 75 miles from Ole Miss which, at that time, looked on Memphis as a second home.

I think it's fair to say that Neyland, one of the greatest coaches in football history, swung a lot of weight in the SEC. He complained to Commissioner Moore, charging that we had offered excessive financial aid to the boys. Charges were also made that Ole Miss was aware that its influential friends had taken the prospects to the 1950 Sugar Bowl game between LSU and Oklahoma.

The axe fell. On August 3, 1950, Commissioner Moore fined Ole Miss a total of $3,000 and ruled the five Memphis boys could not play at Ole Miss or any other SEC schools.

Three other conference members—Louisiana State, Tulane

and Georgia—drew lesser fines on similar grounds involving recruiting. United Press reported the news this way:

> Ole Miss was the main miscreant. Moore fined Mississippi a total of $2,500 for making 'excessive offers of financial aid' to five athletes and an additional $500 for trying to get the jump on its competition by practicing in the summer.

Ole Miss appealed the ruling, but the conference upheld the commissioner. In an interview with Memphis reporters, Ballard, an end at Memphis Tech, said: "I chose the University of Mississippi because it's close to home. There was no money offer made to me. I wish they had."

These troubles were not a simple over-reaction to losing in 1949. Ole Miss, like every other school, was seeking personnel to meet two-platoon demands. The commissioner never substantiated that the staff knew about the Sugar Bowl junket, but he inferred it was part of the recruiting package. It wasn't. What the commissioner got us for was using job proposals. There was no cash involved. It amounted to this: Everett Pidgeon, owner of the Coca-Cola Bottling Company in Memphis and several Mississippi cities, offered summer jobs to the boys. This was something that was being done all over the country. Pidgeon was not an alumnus of Ole Miss. But he helped our athletic program whenever he could, just as he did for Memphis State in his hometown. Overall, the decision was an injustice to the boys and to Ole Miss.

Years later, in a letter to a friend in Memphis, Jimmy Lear of Greenwood, a quarterback who led Ole Miss to some of its greatest triumphs, wrote:

> I was a sophomore in 1950 and we were having a bad season. I think we had won four and lost five, but we beat Mississippi State, and I believe that was the turning point in Vaught's career. That was when he made these rulings: No marriage, no cars, walk to class, walk to practice and no one could go home during football season.
>
> He also said he would not single out any one individual for praise—it was all a team effort. I think that brought us around as a team in 1951 and 1952 better than anything else. We were a close team and a close bunch of boys.

Jimmy may have been right about the turning point. It's important to whip your cross-state rivals in college football, Ole Miss desperately needed to defeat Mississippi State in 1950 if it was going to keep getting the top boys in the state. Going into the State game that year my Rebels needed a victory to prevent a losing season. Just before the game I told the boys:

> Don't worry about getting me fired. You're not going to get me fired. I had a choice of the players in this room or the players over on the Mississippi State side today.
>
> I chose the men in this room. If we can't beat the men on that other team after we've been coaching you three or four years, I don't want to coach any more. If we don't win, I'll quit before they fire me.

They went out and won, 27 to 20.

11

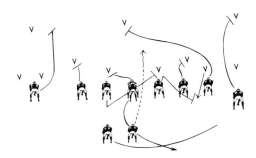

The Tide Turns

A story once circulated that I stood up in church and sang a hymn to impress a family and sign a widely sought prospect. It's a good yarn, but what really happened is better. I was bird hunting at Philadelphia, Mississippi, a few days before Christmas in 1949, when I was summoned to the telephone. The caller was the father of Harol Lofton, a top running back at Brookhaven High School in south Mississippi.

"Coach," he said, "Harol has been exposed enough. He's ready to sign."

That ended my hunting trip. I knew Tulane had been pressing Harol hard, so I got in my car and drove down to Brookhaven. When I got there I discovered Harol wasn't at home. He was singing in a community-wide Christmas cantata at the First Baptist Church. The church had a large sanctuary, but when I got there it was filled. Someone noticed me standing and went and got a cane-bottomed chair and placed it right down front. So, I sat there—a little embarrassed—and looked up at Harol as he sang. I enjoyed the cantata, and

Harol and I left the church together. He played fullback on
our undefeated 1952 team.

The Lofton story points up the fact that Swayze and the
assistant coaches, who work various zones in the state, were
lining up a lot of big, fast athletes—boys who were determined to turn the tide for Ole Miss.

In those days I put a lot of the big boys through "stadium
work"—a physical fitness program where they ran up and
down the steps at Hemingway Stadium to cut off fat and
strengthen their leg muscles. A kid from Hollandale caught
my eye one afternoon.

"Gilbert," I yelled, "you've got a rear end like a $900
mule. You've got a lot of stadium work to get that weight off
you."

The boy was Kline Gilbert, a 245-pound freshman whom
we redshirted—held out of action for a year. He was sitting
on the bench the day Kentucky slaughtered us. In a letter to
James Kingsley, a friend from Tupelo, Kline later wrote:

> I remember the fall of 1949, my redshirt year when Kentucky
> came down to play us. Ole Miss was favored, but Kentucky won, 47
> to 0. They scored every way possible that afternoon. On one occa-
> sion I remember that Billy Mustin had made a nice run, then tried to
> lateral back to another Ole Miss man. A Kentucky boy caught it and
> ran for another touchdown.
>
> Without thinking, I laughed out loud.
>
> I thought Jim Poole was going to kill me. All Vaught did was give
> me a dirty look.
>
> In my sophomore year—1950—I was playing guard and splitting
> time with Egg Young from Tupelo. I had a good game against
> Tulane in New Orleans and was named sophomore lineman of the
> week in the SEC. The following Monday the coaches got on me for
> something that happened in the game, and I shot off my big mouth,
> trying to defend myself. Coach Vaught didn't say a word. But I
> didn't play another minute that year. The coach was right. I guess
> the moral is to keep your mouth shut and eyes and ears open.

Kline may have seen things that way, but I'm confident the
reason he didn't play anymore that season involved more
than speaking up at a squad meeting. The stadium work, plus

summer work in an ice plant at Hollandale, trimmed Gilbert from 245 pounds to 215, and in 1952, he became my first interior lineman to make All-America, an honor I told him he was capable of achieving when we talked about the value of a redshirt year.

Ole Miss didn't set the woods on fire in 1951, but a 6-3-1 record indicated improvement. Othar Crawford, a guard, served as captain, and toward the end of the season, Jim Lear, a senior, began to develop into a slick Split-T quarterback. Twice that year, Ole Miss won national publicity. A big upset and an understandable mistake by a good newsman put us in the spotlight on September 29, 1951—the date the Rebels whipped Kentucky in one of the wildest games ever played in Hemingway Stadium. Clem Brossier, the Associated Press bureau manager in Detroit for many years, will never forget the game. Clem remembers:

I can tell exactly why. I was the Associated Press correspondent in Jackson, Mississippi, at the time and I was covering the game. With about 20 seconds remaining, Ole Miss was ahead of Bear Bryant's great team, 21 to 17. I already had written a hold-for-release lead that Ole Miss had won in a big upset, and I had an open telephone line to New Orleans.

With 20,000 Mississippians in hysteria, Kentucky's brilliant senior quarterback, Babe Parilli, had passed his team 79 yards and seemed unstoppable. As the clock ticked away, Parilli faded back and zipped a pass to tall Jim Proffitt in the end zone. I saw Proffitt reach up and grab the ball, and I saw one official near the sidelines throw up his hands signalling a touchdown.

I hollered into the phone to kill the earlier lead, Kentucky had won. In the press box, which is 80 yards long, there was absolute pandemonium. I turned away from the telephone and started typing a new story. In the confusion in the press box I thought Kentucky had tried to run for the extra point and failed. Keith Fuller, now an assistant general manager with AP in New York, was then in New Orleans at the other end of the telephone line. At my instructions, he had moved a bulletin score:

KENTUCKY 23, OLE MISS 21

Despite all the noise, I heard Keith say, 'Hey, Clem, the radio says Mississippi won.'

I shouted back, 'Like Hell. I saw the touchdown.'

Calmly, Keith's voice came back: 'Clem, look at the scoreboard.'

I did and the damn thing said, 'Ole Miss 21, Kentucky 17.'

When Proffitt caught the pass he was jack-knifed by Pete Mangum's crushing tackle and dropped the ball, which I didn't see. Well, you know how sick something like this makes a wire service reporter.

In its early edition the *Miami Herald* had the score in a box saying Kentucky had won. A few days later I got a letter from a gambler in Miami. He wanted me to make up the $3,000 he said he had paid out. I never answered.

The night after the game while driving back to Jackson my wife and I were listening to music on a radio station up in Memphis. Suddenly, an announcer interrupted the music and I nearly ran off the road. I remember his words well: 'Listen, I'm going to tell all of you just once more. The Associated Press says, Kentucky 23, Ole Miss 21. Don't call me and tell me anything different.' It was about 9:30 at night and the announcer apparently had not seen my corrected story.

Still, Keith Fuller was right in telling me to look at the scoreboard. I guess that's why he's in New York and I'm in Detroit.

The victory over Kentucky and Parilli helped us tremendously. By Sunday, you couldn't find a person who would admit that he wasn't in the stands. That kind of situation helps your team's morale and your recruiting.

Another game that helped to build our national image came on December 1, 1951, at Scott Field in Starkville, the home of Mississippi State. It was the day a football legend was written. No one sitting in the stands that day will ever forget it. I wish Jim Thorpe and Red Grange could have seen the game. In it, Laverne "Showboat" Boykin wrote his own footnote in the history of college football, running for seven touchdowns.

Seven times Lear called one of our bread and butter plays—48 Trap, which sends the fullback up the middle. State was in a wide tackle six. On the first call, Boykin ran 21 yards for a score. On subsequent calls by Lear, it became an automatic touchdown for Boykin, who reeled off additional sprints of 14, 12, 14, 85, 1 and 5 yards.

At the time of this writing, no one has matched that dazzling display by Boykin, who already had his nickname when he arrived at Ole Miss. He had a spectacular high school career at Greenville, a city on the Mississippi River. Seven touchdowns remain an NCAA single-game record for one man. Going into the game, Mississippi State had been ranked tenth nationally on defense. It had a great linebacker-fullback in Joe Fortunato, who went on to become a brilliant All-Pro player with the Chicago Bears. But the day belonged to Boykin and Ole Miss. Lear added 7 extra points to Boykin's 42 and the final score was 49 to 7.

It was a rare day for all of us, and after the game Boykin and his teammates were called back onto the field for pictures. I didn't know it at the time, but up in the stands was Mrs. D. L. Patterson of Greenville. She was Showboat's aunt, and he lived in her home after his parents moved to Columbus. But it was the first time she had seen Boykin play in college. Later, she said:

"I enjoyed that game as much as most older people enjoy ten years!"

12

**Magnificent Rebels Stun
Mighty Maryland, 21-14,
Accept Sugar Bowl Bid**

"The Upset Of
The Year"

The pieces of the puzzle my staff and I had been struggling with fell together in 1952—my sixth season as head coach at Ole Miss. It was what we had been working toward, but an 8-0-2 record was more than we dared dream. After opening with a 54 to 6 win over Memphis State, we tied Kentucky 13-13 and whipped Auburn, 20 to 7. When we tied Vanderbilt, 21-21, I shook up the team a little, making some of the starters take a second row. It worked. The team snapped back, whipping Tulane 20 to 14, Arkansas 34 to 7, LSU 28 to 0 and Houston 6 to 0.

Then we met Jim Tatum's Maryland Terrapins on November 15 in Hemingway Stadium. With Jack Scarbath as its Split-T quarterback, Maryland brought a twenty-two game winning streak to Oxford. My boys were 14 to 20-point underdogs. But our scout, Farley Salmon, the little "Fish" who had led us to an 8-1 season in 1948, detected a weakness in the Maryland defensive line, which had great players including Dick "Little Mo" Modzelewski, who was to play nose-to-nose with our offensive tackle, Kline Gilbert. Salmon had noticed that Modzelewski and the other front men would split according to the offensive alinement.

We decided to widen our splits a little, figuring that our backs could strike quickly up the middle. We were right. The headlines in Sunday's newspapers told the story:

Magnificent Rebels Stun
Mighty Maryland, 21-14;
Accept Sugar Bowl Bid

My boys won the game the hard way. We scored three touchdowns against the nation's No. 1 defensive team, but on four other occasions we got inside the Terps' five-yard line. This team, with Lear—"King Lear"—at quarterback had spirit, courage and togetherness. The team could have folded after I made a mistake, a very costly one. As a coach you never quite know how you let a situation get out of hand, but it can happen. Late in the first quarter Ole Miss had stopped Maryland on our own 46 yard line. On fourth down with three to go, Bernie Faloney went back to kick for Maryland.

I sent in a back to return the punt but I violated the 30-second rule. He got in late. The five yard penalty gave Maryland a first down on our 41. Six plays later Chet Hanulak, aided by a great fake by Scarbath, turned our right end for 11 yards and a touchdown.

Ole Miss didn't fold. With Lear working smoothly, handing off to Dick Westerman, Wilson Dillard and Harol Lofton and passing to Westerman and Bud Slay, Ole Miss moved 83 yards in thirteen plays. A busted signal at the Maryland 12 cost us two yards, but Lear more than got it back. Bud Howell sneaked into the northeast corner between Dick Nolan and Bob Destefano and Lear threw a strike for a touchdown, then kicked it 7-7.

Nolan repaid us. He ran the kickoff back 90 yards for a touchdown. But this only aroused my boys. There was no way to know it at the time, but there would be no more big plays for Maryland. Ole Miss kept striking at the holes in the Maryland line and in the fourth quarter Wilson Dillard scored twice. When the game ended Kline Gilbert came to the bench with two black eyes after one hell of a day of blocking. When Modzelewski received the Outland Award as the year's top lineman, he said Gilbert was the best blocker he ever met.

Actually, except for two big plays by Maryland, the game was all ours. Ole Miss outrushed Maryland, 197 yards to 95. Lear passed for 231 yards. Maryland managed only 33 and Scarbath completed his first pass with just 1:14 left in the game. It was a great team effort, with boys like Crawford Mims, Henry Linton, Jimmy Patton, Jack Reed, Lea Paslay, Ed Beatty, Marvin Trauth, Jim Caldwell, Jerry May and Red Muirhead joining those I've already mentioned. In his own incisive style, Walter Stewart wrote:

> If there had been an ounce of cur in the Ole Miss team, it would have sent a yellow bubble to the surface half a dozen times. After driving Maryland to its heels early in conflict, the Rebs held Maryland snugly for three downs—and the Terps kicked. But Ole Miss had delayed the game and the penalty gave the Terps a first down and placed the bit between teeth whose gums were beginning to bleed.

> Maryland scored. A team with dough in the heart would have whimpered something about bad luck and folded. Ole Miss dabbed at the wound and went barreling down into the end zone for seven and seven. The Rebs were in the saddle and yipping gaily.

> Again and again the Rebels stormed to the gates of glory. Again and again they fell back empty-handed and dazed with effort. An interception—a fumble—a poor handoff. But back they came, shaking off the dark vapors and driving with a right matchless bravery.

> Until at last their descending sword caught defense along the grain—split it wide—split it wide again and this portion of the globe went up in epic sound. This triumph is a resounding tribute to Coach John Vaught and his crafty staff—to a football team which for a day was without parallel. It is a tribute to a student body with character sufficient to spawn this band of anvil-handed smithers. Long may they live and richly may they prosper.

In *The Clarion-Ledger*, Mississippi's largest newspaper, Wayne Thompson wrote:

> King Jimmy Lear, playing the greatest football game of his brilliant college career, led the Ole Miss Rebels to the gridiron heights here this sun-kissed Saturday afternoon as he sparked these Rebels to a 21 to 14 victory.
>
> Not since the Mississippi State Maroons put the Magnolia state on the football map with its 13 to 7 victory over Army in 1935 has a Mississippi football team reached the peak that it did here Saturday afternoon.

Carl Walters, the dean of Mississippi sportswriters, looked at the upset this way in the *Jackson Daily News:*

> This particular game was the most thrilling that we have ever seen... Also—and of major importance—it was the most significant victory ever recorded by a Mississippi football team. This win by the Rebels over a club like Maryland will mean more favorable publicity for the University of Mississippi and the State of Mississippi—so far as football is concerned—than anything that has even been written into the record books.
>
> This great Ole Miss victory is now history, but it will be talked about and "played over" for days and weeks and months and years to come. And if you were not among those present at Hemingway Stadium last Saturday afternoon, we suggest that you go off to a nice, quiet spot and give yourself a good kicking, Joe, because you missed out on the biggest and best game in Mississippi football annals.

After the game the telephone rang in the fieldhouse. It was the Sugar Bowl calling with the first bid Ole Miss had ever received from that great New Year's Day attraction.

In the Maryland dressing room, Coach Tatum, who had been freshman coach at North Carolina when I coached the varsity line, said, "If Maryland had to lose, I had rather lose to Coach Vaught, a great coach, than anyone I can think of."

Unfortunately, the comments didn't stop there. After he took his team back to College Park, Tatum ran into a lot of criticism, especially from H. C. "Curly" Byrd, a long-time coach who had become president of the University of

Maryland. Soon, Jim began criticizing the officiating, his team and himself. In one interview he said his first team took the day off, adding: "And I didn't give them any help from the bench. For instance, every time Mississippi got near our goal I sat there praying they wouldn't score instead of telling Scarbath on the sidelines what to do in case they didn't."

President Byrd remarked that if "Tatum had done as much coaching in November as he did in September and October, we wouldn't have lost a game." It should be noted that the loss to Ole Miss was a temporary derailment. In 1953 Tatum would coach Maryland to a national title. One of his 10 victims would be Ole Miss.

But the victory in 1952 at Oxford boosted our own national image. Ole Miss jumped to sixth place in the Associated Press weekly poll, breaking into the Top 10 for the first time. The 32,500 fans—at that time the largest crowd in the history of Mississippi football—who saw the upset went wild. On the way out of the stadium a few alumni pitched dollar bills into windows at the fieldhouse. I was shocked. The sports world was shocked by our win. Ole Miss' victory over Maryland was voted the Sports Upset of the Year by the Associated Press. These were the major upsets in 1952:

1. Mississippi over Maryland
2. Notre Dame over Oklahoma
3. Iowa over Ohio State
4. Notre Dame over Southern Cal
5. Sexias over Sedgman
6. Boros winning U. S. Open
7. Ashenfelter winning Steeplechase
8. Pitt over Notre Dame
9. Steelers over New York Giants
10. St. John's over Kentucky.

Our little school would experience its share of bumps, but some mighty golden years were just down the road for Ole Miss.

13

The Golden Years

I've never met Charles Cates of Murfreesboro, Tennessee, but I've heard about him. Cates got up early on the morning of November 16, 1957, and drove 240 miles to Memphis to see his favorite football team—the University of Tennessee—play Ole Miss in Crump Stadium. As the afternoon wore on, he began to pay more and more attention to the PA system announcer, who Cates decided was a frustrated TV sports-caster. Even in the second half, the announcer insisted on telling the name of each tackler.

Early in the third quarter, Tennessee tried a wide sweep to the left and the announcer intoned: "Tackle by Hickerson." The next play went wide to the right and the announcer said: "Tackle by Hickerson." That was too much for Cates.

"Tackle by Hickerson, hell!" he exclaimed. "There's no man alive who could have done that. What's that announcer trying to do, make Hickerson an All-American off one game?"

E. B. Blackburn, a Memphian who knew Cates and a little about Ole Miss football, smiled and told Cates the tackles weren't made by the same man, noting that Gene Hickerson was playing on the right side and his younger brother, Willie, was on the left. Ole Miss' family approach to football dismayed Cates.

"Two of them? Hell, I give up!"

Cates got up then and there and drove back to Murfreesboro. The final score was 14 to 7, Ole Miss.

Three years later, when Ole Miss was on its way to a national championship, *Time* magazine, in its November 28, 1960, edition, said:

> By bigtime football standards, the whole operation seems as pleasantly relaxed as a backyard barbecue. The players are almost all home-state boys. They perform in a modest stadium before informal crowds that are packed with friends and relatives. . .But year in and year out, the University of Mississippi plays some of the finest football in the nation. . . Coach Vaught is a shrewd and patient recruiter. To hear him talk, Ole Miss football is a family affair.

Well, I hope Ole Miss football always remains a family affair. If we have any secrets, that's one of them.

Many observers feel that Ole Miss football began its golden years—winning most of its games and building a national image and following—in 1952. It certainly was a pivotal year. The achievements of the boys on the field wore well with our students and supporters. Their pride matched that of the boys. Everyone likes to reach the mountain peaks.

Looking back, dramatic turns for the school became commonplace in 1952. An Ole Miss "M" Club Alumni Association—made up of graduated sports letter winners—was organized and my good friend, Shed Hill Roberson Sr. of Clarksdale, served as the first president. Today, this group gives an annual $500 All-America scholarship to the university and promotes the spring Awards Banquet. It also gives us one more recruiting link across the state.

One of the most significant events in Ole Miss history also took place in 1952—a gift of $500,000 from R. M. "Bob" Carrier. Known as "Mr. Bob" to everyone, he loved Ole Miss and its football teams. A millionaire lumberman-sportsman, he had indicated more than once that he would do whatever was necessary to help us.

Chancellor J. D. Williams, on several occasions, had spoken to me about the need for a better engineering school. The subject was close to my own mind. Ole Miss had been losing some good athletes because it didn't have the proper engineering facilities. Once during a visit, Bob brought up the question of a major donation to Ole Miss. The athletic department needed a dormitory for its players, but I made a pitch for the engineering school. I'm sure that Chancellor Williams and others also had told Bob of this need. All of us were elated when he gave a half million dollars to build Carrier Hall, an excellent engineering building.

Bob Carrier was an alumnus of Cornell but he thought the world of Ole Miss football. Born in Brookville, Pennsylvania, on May 16, 1876, Bob came to Sardis, Mississippi, in 1900 and entered the hardwood lumber business. He made a fortune in it, and he lived at Barnacre, an antebellum plantation home. Barnacre is the center of a nationally known wildlife preserve, and I hunted there with Bob, who was one fine man. It has been my observation over the years that loose talk always tags after money. In that regard, Tom Siler had this to say in the *Saturday Evening Post* on October 13, 1956:

> There inevitably has been gossip that Carrier is a financial angel to the football team too. But all the gossips can do is cite a warm friendship that exists between Carrier and Vaught, as well as Carrier's strong interest in football—he frequently attended Ole Miss practice sessions in his more active days. There is no evidence that the school has been guilty of illegal payments to athletes.

Siler, the biographer of General Robert Neyland and University of Tennessee football, hit the target. The simple truth is, you can't buy friendship or winners.

Bob Carrier died on September 12, 1957, but his gifts— after Carrier Hall was built he set up an additional $500,000 scholarship fund for deserving Mississippians—helped the university and the athletic department tremendously. Thanks to him, Ole Miss was able to recruit Richard Ross, a fine center on our teams in the early 1960's. When he graduated in 1963, Richard, an electrical engineer, went to work in the Computer Center at the university. At night, long after the regular programmers had gone home, Richard tinkered with the computer. He taught himself how to feed data into it. Soon, he was experimenting with football information. Meanwhile, word got around about Ross' abilities and he became the center's director. One day Richard came up to me and said: "Coach, why don't you use the computer for your scouting reports? I think you'll be surprised how much it can tell you." I wish that I could write that I jumped at the chance—but I didn't. I was the usual skeptical John. I dragged my feet for about a year. But Richard Ross refused to give up. He wanted to help Ole Miss football and he finally convinced me in 1964 that the computer could do just that. I'm glad that he did. It gave us a jump on most SEC schools. Now, we use it to tell us things about ourselves as well as other teams. In 1969, the computer told us we should make some changes in our defense. And we did.

It was one of the saddest days in my life when Richard and his brother, Tony, lost their lives in a plane crash at Norwood, Louisiana, on December 19, 1969. But the contributions of Richard Ross and Bob Carrier to Ole Miss will never die. Future students will share in their legacies. To me, these men—one with wealth and the other with an idea—reflect the value of athletics to an educational institution. I like to win, I coached to win; but the important thing to remember is this: Ole Miss built a successful football program because it got the right kind of boys—and most of them from Mississippi or nearby states.

We have physical guidelines in our recruiting, and we know they are important. But a coach, perhaps more than anyone else, knows he is dealing with boys, not robots. If a boy qualifies inside himself, he can become a winner despite physical shortcomings. Bill Basham of Paducah, Kentucky, which is closer to Ole Miss than Biloxi, fits into that category. To use a label to help make a point, Bill might be called the heroic "12th man" on our 1960 national championship team, which had a lot of tremendous athletes.

Some of his teammates called Bill "Foggy," saying he mixed the signals a lot. In practices, our quarterbacks occasionally would call a play, then tease Basham by saying: "Is that okay with you, Foggy?"

That kind of kidding didn't bother Bill. He had a lot of intelligence and pride. He dedicated himself to Ole Miss football. A guard, Basham had to take a second row to two talented boys, Richard Price and Warner Alford. As a result, Bill failed to make the traveling squad when Ole Miss opened the 1960 season at Houston on September 17. In the first half against a tough Cougar squad, the Rebels lost six linemen to injuries. I was beginning to worry when Doc Varner came up to me just before the half and said, "Foggy's over there on the bench." I went over and told him to go get dressed. Later, I learned that Bill, a Navy reservist, had flown to Houston in a Navy plane from Memphis, then thumbed a ride to the stadium.

You have probably guessed the ending. Basham played the finest 30 minutes of football in his life. On the first play of the third quarter, he forced a Houston fumble. Ole Miss went on to a 42-0 win, an important step in a 9-0-1 season. The Bill Basham story is a reminder that the history of Ole Miss football from 1947 to 1970 is a bit more than rounding up of super-athletes. Desire has its place.

"Move the ball. Move the ball." Francis Schmidt preached that to me at TCU, and I think the Ole Miss attack since 1947 would put a smile on his face. I still have the playbook he gave me. Ole Miss has used just about everything except the old Swinging Gate formation. Our offense has gotten the job done with the Notre Dame Box, the Split-T, the Winged-T, the I-formation and our own specialty—the quarterback sprint out.

Maybe it's my age telling on me, but from time to time I used to read in the newspapers—especially after close games that Ole Miss lost—that I became too conservative. What the critics forget is the caliber of the opposition. A few coaches have said, "Vaught is from the old school. He gets the best personnel possible and says 'I'm coming after you.' It's a question of strength against strength and since he annually gets some of the best athletes in the South he figures Ole Miss will win."

That's interesting, but the truth goes deeper. If a team thinks Ole Miss doesn't make intelligent changes on offense and defense it's going to be beaten. I think Coach Billy Murphy of Memphis State detected our approach to football as well as anyone when he said: "You think you are seeing the same Olè Miss attack until after the game and you start looking at films to see where your defense broke down. Suddenly, while you are sitting there looking at the movies, you realize Ole Miss has made subtle changes—that you've been beaten by a multiple or Houston offense, not a winged-T."

If I make any comment on that I might give away a secret or two that I'm not quite ready to divulge. But some things, of course, are self-evident. For a long, long time, Ole Miss has been known as a team with a quarterback-fullback offense. When we have a good combination there, we move the football.

Statistics belong to computers, mathematicians and rainy days—I'm more interested in the human element—but Southeastern Conference figures reveal that between 1948 and 1968 Ole Miss led the SEC in total offense by three country miles. In 207 games, Ole Miss rushed 43,632 yards and passed for 25,123, a total of 68,755 yards. A fast divider on my staff tells me that is a little more than 39 miles. Alabama came in second in that 21-season span, gaining 61,192 yards in 216 games. That's about 36 miles.

What about the Ole Miss defense? Well, Coach Buster Poole and his boys limited our opponents to 45,363 yards, which proved stingy enough for first place. Again, Alabama came in second. The nicest thing about all these figures is that they can be converted into five SEC championships—1954, 1955, 1960, 1962 and 1963.

Personally, I'm convinced that the best years are still to come at Ole Miss, but I can understand the thinking of sportswriters and others who feel the Rebel football program peaked between 1959 and 1963—five seasons in which Ole Miss won one national championship and lost only two games, both of them to LSU by a total of seven points.

It should be clear that Louisiana State has been something of a thorn to me since 1932, when the Tigers tied the Horned Frogs I captained, 3-3. But my Mississippians have tried to pay LSU back in kind, and I think a careful review of the record will reveal that they have been more successful than not.

Where does Ole Miss find its talent? We have found that you can't overlook any place—cities or cross-roads towns. Ole Miss signed big Johnny Brewer, a fine end for us and an All-Pro linebacker, out of a little school at Redwood after seeing him play basketball. Just as Swayze had done in Gene Hickerson's case, we signed Brewer on his size and potential.

Larry Grantham, an end who could get into trouble on defense and get out of it quicker than a cat, won a scholarship because our recruiters had seen him play baseball. Larry might not have gone on to his tremendous career with the New York Jets if he had not been part of the team togetherness that we deem essential at Ole Miss. A vote of the squad returned him to the team in his senior year after dismissal for breaking a rule.

A coach must have—must demand—strict adherence to rules and regulations, but a compassion for a boy and an understanding of his problems are never out of order. My door was always open to my players. Newsmen did, but players didn't have to check with my secretary, Mrs. Faye Parker, and go through an appointment calendar.

Some skeptics laughed when I told a newsman in May of 1963 that when a boy comes to Ole Miss to play and quits there is something wrong with the boy. At first glance, that may sound a little pompous on my part. But our No. 1 objective is morale. Football is a psychological game, and the staff spends considerable time trying to have a happy situation for the team.

The best boys play. It's all based on competition. We tell a boy if he's best he's going to play. If not, he's going to have to take a second row.

Now football players are people, that's for sure. At one time or another, some of my greatest players, including at least three All-Americans, thought about leaving Ole Miss. The list includes Charley Conerly, Kline Gilbert, Eagle Day, Glynn Griffing, Marvin Trauth, Red Ott, Vernon Studdard and others.

Sometimes, these thoughts come because a boy has to take a second row, but usually something else is involved— courtship, problems at home and other personal crises. I try to understand the problems; I spend a lot of time with the boys. Quite often, things can be worked out. Once a player leaves the team, it takes a lot of courage for him to go before his teammates and ask to be reinstated.

I have seen some awfully big boys stand there and cry. But boys who leave and never come back can't help Ole Miss. Those who left but changed their minds have.

Ole Miss football players stand tall, and it is no accident. Early in my talks with Swayze, I told him, "Tom, let's look for linemen 6-3 or taller." Later, I told him to keep a sharp eye out for tall quarterbacks. It's much easier that way than trying to use elevator shoes. Now Tom's file doesn't explain why we like tall boys, but the reason is simple. If you take an exceptionally tall athlete that hasn't filled out and reached his potential and put him on Isometric exercises, you can build his strength. And when he adds the extra weight that goes with strength he can still get into a blocking stance without any trouble. A 5-11 boy weighing 200 pounds will have trouble if he adds weight and strength. I think Ole Miss set the guideline for the tall tackles that pro teams now utilize.

In his index file, Swayze keeps data on each potential recruit in the state of Mississippi. The cards, in addition to the usual biographical and school information, have a place for these notations: Yes, No, and Check Back. If a boy gets an unqualified "yes" on his card, we go all out to sign him. It means he has the physical and mental capabilities that we have to have. A "no" is jotted down when a boy tells us that he would like to play football at Ole Miss but isn't really interested in an education. To give him a scholarship makes about as much sense as giving yourself a headache.

Sometimes, a "no" is put opposite a name if the boy seems to lack aggressiveness. We have found that if a boy doesn't want to get back up after getting knocked down he can't play at Ole Miss. I guess my attitude about that goes back to 1932 when Harrison Stafford nearly killed me.

Ole Miss has been extremely fortunate in finding a lot of rangy football players with speed and agility—men who can run 40 yards—"the football forty"—in under five seconds. We send a representative to each track meet of any consequence in the state. Swayze, who uses the assistant coaches as a check against his own thinking, keeps many high school boys in the "check back" bracket.

Follow-ups are important. That's why Buster Poole signed Jake Gibbs out of John Rundle High School in Grenada. Everyone knew that Jake was a fine baseball player, but his size—5-10 and 160 pounds—worried us. Jake, however, had that inner something that makes an athlete. Our signing of him has to be a bit of a coup. His brother was at Mississippi State at the time, but the staff there dallied at least one day longer than we about his size. Jake, of course, grew to almost six feet and 180 pounds and became an All-American quarterback as well as an All-American baseball player.

One of Jimmy Lear's high school coaches at Greenwood— not Carl Maddox, who coached him his final two years and is now the athletic director at LSU—told us Jimmy wasn't aggressive enough for college football. That opinion went into Swayze's file, but subsequent check backs convinced

Swayze that Lear would be an aggressive leader. Tom was right. When Lear quarterbacked for us—especially in the big game with Maryland when he outdueled Jack Scarbath—he was in complete command. Finding such winners has to be one of our secrets.

The importance of home-state ties won us Glynn Griffing, the first graduate of little Culkin High School to win a major college scholarship. Paul Dietzel of the University of South Carolina was the coach at LSU back then, and he wanted Griffing. Culkin, which is near Vicksburg, is closer to Baton Rouge than it is to Ole Miss.

"I really wanted to go to LSU at first," Glynn told me later. "One morning Paul Dietzel walked into the house before breakfast. Mother fixed him bacon and eggs and he certainly impressed me. He can talk. When he left, Dietzel said, 'Glynn, I've got a bunk at LSU with your name on it.' "

"I told him, 'I'll be there'. I drove a bus to school in my senior year and when I got home late that afternoon I still was excited about going to LSU. My parents had other ideas. Dietzel hadn't convinced them. My father said, 'Glynn, if you are going to live in Mississippi you ought to go to school in Mississippi.' Dad turned my thinking around. He worked with a graduate of Mississippi State and I believe he really wanted me to go to Starkville. But I visited both campuses and something about the attitude and dress of the athletes at Ole Miss impressed me most. You could see immediately that you would have to compete with good boys. I guess it was that challenge that brought me to Ole Miss."

Chalk one up for our family affair. Family and state ties can work against you when you leave your own area. That's why I lost some good players to Dietzel and LSU. One boy stands out in my mind—Pat Screen, who played for New Orleans Jesuit. In 1960 I invited Pat to the campus for the LSU game. I didn't see him, but they tell me that Screen jumped up and started cheering when Jerry Stovall broke loose on a long run for LSU. Now if that happened, there was a boy who had come to Mississippi but left his heart in Louisiana.

I matched wits with Dietzel many other times, and one of the memorable ones involved Perry Lee Dunn of Natchez. LSU really went after him. But, a couple of days before signing time in December, I invited Perry Lee and his father to the campus. Then we went on a hunting trip and we kept moving. On the day before you could sign in the SEC we decided to drive to Jackson and spend the night at a hotel there. I signed Perry Lee at one minute after midnight. At that hour, Paul sat at the Dunn home in Natchez.

The reputation of high school football players in Mississippi began to attract other coaches in the late 1940's and has continued. Frank Broyles of Arkansas frequently visited the state while an assistant at Georgia Tech. Army kept an eye on Mississippi too. One day in 1954, Raymond Brown was practicing basketball at Greenville when two men wearing Air Force blue walked into the gym. Ray told me later: "I practically fell on the floor in my hurry to shake hands with one of them—Doc Blanchard. Captain Blanchard identified the other man as Bobby Dobbs and said they had flown in from West Point in a jet trainer just to see me. I gave a lot of thought to going to the Academy, but my father had died and I didn't want to go too far away from my mother. I also was interested in law, and I knew Ole Miss had a good law school as well as good football."

When I got to Greenville, Ray was ready to sign with us. He became an excellent quarterback and the only player ever to be chosen the Most Valuable Player in a Sugar Bowl game by unanimous vote. Ray played a couple of seasons with the Baltimore Colts, but he stuck to his goal. He's an attorney in Pascagoula.

The more I reflect on it, I think I arrived in Mississippi at the right time. Bruiser Kinard once said:

> Until the middle 40's, high school football in Mississippi hadn't developed as it should have. We were 20 years behind Texas, New Jersey, Ohio and Pennsylvania. Then all of a sudden we began to produce good football players. Things began to fall together and that prompted us to stay in the state and recruit. As long as the supply

meets the demand, we won't venture too far from home. One big
factor in our favor has been the improvement in high school football.

Our alumni got together too. Jeff Hamm, who is retired now
but was our business manager for athletics for many years, told
me that the alumni were split so badly in the 1920's that he
had doors slammed in his face. From 1912 to 1926, fraterni-
ties were banned at Ole Miss, but Hamm said they existed sub
rosa and this had a lot to do with the factional fights. Jeff
thinks a winning football program unified our alumni more
than any other single thing.

Actually, there are many things that contribute to a successful athletic program; physical facilities can't be overlooked.
Mississippi has come a long way since the football staff sat in
cars to make game plans. An athletic dormitory, Miller Hall—
named for Martin Miller—was opened in September of 1959.
Until that time, our athletes had been scattered in Vardaman
and Mayes halls. Miller Hall houses 122 athletes. In the near
future, Ole Miss hopes to have a new athletic dorm which will
accommodate 250 athletes. After much hard work by Tad
Smith, Ole Miss got a two-million-dollar coliseum in 1966. It
seats 8,500 for basketball and will accommodate 10,000 for
academic and social events. The old cow pasture—Hemingway
Stadium—isn't the same either. A cow would starve on it. In
1970 we installed an all-weather artificial turf.

Every Ole Miss team since 1947 has used a man-in-motion
series. It means some back is on the move, keeping the enemy
defense off balance or guessing. We had these motion plays
when Conerly was the tailback in the Notre Dame Box. We
continued them in 1948 when Fish Salmon ignited the
Split-T for us.

Since 1948 we have used some variation of the Split-T,
although the Winged-T was a better name in the late 1950's
and early 1960's. On occasion we have used the Straight T
and the drop back pass. In 1968, after the University of
Texas-El Paso bruised us with them in the Sun Bowl, we
added flankers to our attack.

Ole Miss likes to use a free-wheeling offense, and the quarterback sprint came into being in 1954 with Herman "Eagle" Day, a kid who made as much progress at quarterback as any I have ever coached. Eagle had a good arm—he pitched five no-hitters in high school baseball—but when he arrived at Ole Miss he was just about as green a football player as you can imagine. But we started our sprint out patterns—where the quarterback rolls left or right at a 45-degree angle from the line of scrimmage—with Eagle.

Some authorities give Ole Miss credit for "inventing" the sprint-out, and we're happy about that. To us, it seemed a natural progression from the Split or Sliding-T attack, where the quarterback moves down the line right at the heels of his blockers. Our sprint-out, with its 45-degree slant, gives the quarterback extra depth. Using it, he can recognize the pressure points better. Once he gets outside, he knows when to turn up or throw. The good sprint-out man has to have quickness and ability to accelerate, especially if he decides to turn upfield.

In a lot of ways, Eagle was the original Mississippi gambler at quarterback. I'll never forget the 1956 Cotton Bowl when Eagle and Ole Miss were up against TCU and its All-American back, Jim Swink. My mother was still living then, and she came over from Fort Worth with Uncle Edell and other members of the family. She had a good seat along the 50-yard line with Jeff Hamm and other Ole Miss people.

With three minutes to go in the game, Ole Miss had a fourth down on its own 45 yard line. I thought about punting, but Eagle would not look at the sidelines. He rolled out to his left and at the last moment—and under great pressure— tossed a pass to Paige Cothren, our fullback, for a first down. A few plays later Billy Lott took it in for a touchdown, and Ole Miss won, 14 to 13.

"Heck, I didn't want to punt," Eagle said when he came to a cheering bench. I decided it would serve no purpose to chastise him for not looking at me.

Eagle and I always had a little trouble communicating. In fact, Eagle, a part-Choctaw Indian from Columbia, cured me

of verbal signals from the sidelines. He is the reason I remember the Georgia game in 1955 so well. We won it in Atlanta,
26 to 13, but it was a trying night. It was illegal at the time,
but I would shout plays to Eagle. The noise that night was
tremendous and my shouts were lost in the din. Eagle tried to
pick them up, but, unfortunately, the calls all started with an
"S." When I shouted for a slant, Eagle would screen. It went
that way all night. But team execution went well despite the
mixups. I don't know what would have happened otherwise.
The boys won by doing just the opposite of what their coach
called. I decided then and there to quit shouting.

Eagle was one of the most sensitive kids I ever coached.
Once, against Arkansas, he was rolling out when someone on
the staff shouted, "Quit dancing and start running!" Eagle, a
sophomore, heard that shout. He got so upset about it that
he skipped our Sunday night meeting. He went to a friend's
room—Freddy Phillips from Purvis—and talked about leaving
Ole Miss.

This happened in 1953 just before the Maryland game at
College Park, and Johnny Cain, our backfield coach, finally
found Eagle, who was a sophomore. I think Johnny tried to
give Eagle an out when he asked, "Eagle, why didn't you
come to the meeting? You were sleeping, weren't you?"

But the boy was honest.

"No, sir," he said. "I just didn't want to come."

Cain brought him to my office.

"Aren't you thinking about Maryland, Eagle?" I asked.

"No, sir. How can I think about a team when I don't get to
play much and when I do someone yells at me?"

I sent him back to his room. But I took him to Maryland.
Eagle warmed the bench in the first half, and Maryland, on
its way to a national championship, took us apart. At the
half, I asked the other quarterbacks what they would like to
do differently, but they didn't say much. Finally, Eagle
spoke up: "Coach, why don't we open up on them? We
ought to sprint-out on first down."

Turning to him, I said, "You ready to play?"

After the Maryland game, Eagle became a dedicated boy, one of our best.

In 1955, Ole Miss faced its usual tough battle with LSU in Baton Rouge. On the bus to the stadium, I sat by Eagle and we had a long talk. I wanted to build his confidence. Later, in a newspaper interview that took place after Day had spent 13 seasons as a pro player in Canada and the United States, Eagle recalled that ride:

> Coach Vaught sat by me on the bus when I was a senior heading for my last game against LSU, and he said, 'Eagle, I want to tell you something. I want you to throw anytime you want to tonight.'
>
> That gave me the confidence, the green light that I needed. Cold chills ran over me, but once the game started I was a new man. Previously, I had been reluctant to throw deep in our own territory. But not after that bus ride. Vaught made me a passer in that game with LSU, which we won, 29 to 26.

It was a clear case of a kid finding himself. The best way for a coach to get into trouble is to forget that each player is an individual. Eagles must fly.

There are so many faces, so many teams to recall in these recollections that it's impossible to give them all the credit they are due. That's why every letterman is listed in this book.

Some things, of course, stand out more than others. How could I ever forget Ray Brown's 92-yard run against Texas in the 1958 Sugar Bowl game? It had started as a punt, but a Texas boy broke through and Ray decided to run. By the time he got to the other end of the field, Ray was staggering, but he kept a death-clutch on the football. Running right at Ray's heels was Jackie Simpson, our All-American guard who had been a high school fullback, pleading:

"Throw me the ball! Throw me the ball! Dammit, let me score just once!"

"I would have tossed it to him," Ray said, "but I was so tired I was afraid I would fumble it away."

Going into that game, Ole Miss had lost twice in the Sugar

Bowl—to Georgia Tech and Navy. But in 1958 the boys decided the school had been embarrassed enough. Texas fell, 39 to 7.

That game with Texas jogs my memory about another matter, too. It involves conference ties and ethics. I am a strong believer in the Southeastern Conference. When an SEC team plays a school from another conference I want our team to win—and that includes Mississippi State. In our last game of 1957, State tied us, 7-7, and while we were preparing for Texas, Coach Wade Walker of State let an assistant, Leonard McCullough, go to Austin to help Darrell Royal and his team prepare for us. I don't like that sort of thing. Actually, I don't think the results were complimentary to State. Over the years, though, our relationship with State has been an excellent one despite our competition for football players.

The Associated Press acclaimed the 1959 Ole Miss squad the "Team of the Decade" in the Southeastern Conference. I'll buy that. It was one fine squad, scoring 329 points for a school record. It gave up only 21. That team lost the famous 7–3 heart-stopper to LSU, the defending national champs, but in the rematch in the Sugar Bowl Ole Miss won going away, 21-0. Billy Cannon, who had shot us down with a brilliant punt return in the first game, gained only eight yards.

Both LSU and Ole Miss had just about as good defensive units as college football has ever seen, but our junior quarterback, Jake Gibbs, ruined the day for LSU 38 seconds before the first half ended. Jake hit Cowboy Woodruff with a 43-yard scoring strike right down the middle and there went the old ball game.

The 1959 team had the poise and depth that great football teams need. Actually, I don't think it had a weakness. There wasn't a dumb boy in the group. Our fullback, Charlie Flowers, won Academic All-America honors, and there were many honor students playing with him. Ole Miss put two men on the first All-America team—Flowers and Marvin Terrell, a magnificent guard who was voted Lineman of the Year in the SEC. In the key quarterback-fullback area, the team was three deep, actually four deep in some cases. Bobby Franklin, a senior, headed the quarterbacks, but that little trophy hunter—he won the Most Valuable award in the 1958 Gator Bowl and in the 1960 Sugar Bowl—found himself pushed by Gibbs, Doug Elmore and Billy Brewer.

Flowers couldn't afford to take a day off, either. Right behind him was Jim Anderson, a hard runner.

I think the 1959 team enjoyed playing football as much as any squad I ever saw. It had fun doing a good job. The boys knew they were good, and were proud of it. They handled some teams so easily that from time to time they would pull a stunt or two on the field. In the Tennessee game in Memphis, the boys found they could do just about what they wanted to do with the Vols, so they decided to try a quick kick, a Tennessee trademark back in the Neyland era. Well, it backfired. The Lord only knows why, but the boys decided to let Flowers, a left-footer, try it. Tennessee partially blocked it, and finally got a score out of it. Ole Miss won, 37-7.

Many of the boys on that team distinguished themselves in pro football. In addition to those I've already mentioned, there were many other great players—Bobby Crespino, Larry Grantham, Johnny Brewer, Ken Kirk, Richard Price, Butch Kempinska, Robert Owens, Ralph Smith, Jerry Daniels, George Blair, Billy Ray Jones, Fred Lentjes, Bob Khayat, John Robinson, Warner Alford, Rush McKay, Dewey Partridge, Art Doty, Bob Benton, Jerry Brown and Shed Hill Roberson Jr.

Here's their record:

1959

September 19	Houston	16-0
September 26	Kentucky	16-0
October 3	Memphis State	43-0
October 10	Vanderbilt	33-0
October 17	Tulane	53-7
October 24	Arkansas	28-0
October 31	LSU	3-7
November 7	Chattanooga	58-0
November 14	Tennessee	37-7
November 28	Mississippi State	42-0

There were a number of holdovers from the 1959 team, and Ole Miss won its first national title in 1960 with a 9-0-1 record and a 14 to 6 victory over Rice in the Sugar Bowl. This was the team that whipped Arkansas, 10 to 7, on Allen Green's controversial field goal in Little Rock. The next week we played LSU at Oxford in a televised game, and the Tigers had us whipped, 6-3, with just six seconds left.

Incredibly, Green bailed us out with a tremendous 41-yard field goal. I don't know how many heart failures there were in Hemingway Stadium that afternoon.

Our quarterback, Gibbs, won All-American honors in 1960, and Brewer and Price joined him on the first All-Southeastern team. The Football Writers Association of America selected Ole Miss as national champs, a decision that brought the *Look* magazine—Grantland Rice trophy to the south for the first time. Here's the record of that fine team:

1960

September 17	Houston	42-0
September 24	Kentucky	21-6
October 1	Memphis State	31-20
October 8	Vanderbilt	26-0
October 15	Tulane	26-13
October 22	Arkansas	10-7
October 29	LSU	6-6
November 5	Chattanooga	45-0
November 12	Tennessee	24-3
November 26	Mississippi State	35-9

Practically all of our games with LSU have matched the intenseness of our recruiting battles. As every sports fan knows, the Tigers are extremely popular in Louisiana, but it was Ole Miss that took part in the first sellout in the history of Tiger Stadium, which seats 67,500. That was in 1958, when Ole Miss had a strong team but LSU was on its way to a national championship. I'd like to skip the score, but it was LSU, 14 to 0.

Airplanes got into the act in 1959. There were newspapers reports that LSU was saturated with "Go to Hell, LSU" leaflets. A newsman called me to ask about Ole Miss students pulling such a stunt.

I told him I thought Paul Dietzel, who had been in the Army Air Corps, had given up flying. The problem in an LSU-Ole Miss game is to keep emotions down. You don't need to psyche the kids.

I have often said that my Ole Miss teams are only as good as the seniors. They carry the responsibility. That goes off the field as well as on it. We have a "big brother" system at Ole Miss, with the seniors and juniors keeping an eye on the younger boys. Bobo Uzzle, a defensive end, was Archie Manning's big brother. Once, in his freshman year, Archie failed to make up Bobo's bed, and Uzzle got out the paddle. But, before Archie came in, Bobo met another lineman, Alan Bush, and told him, "I'm going to put the board to Archie."

"Listen, Bobo," Bush said, "defensive ends are dime a dozen, and you know how Coach Vaught has been looking for a good quarterback since 1964."

Archie escaped the paddle. Togetherness!

Recognizing the different temperaments of boys is essential to successful coaching. Each athlete must be handled a little differently. Once, in the early 1960s, we had two All-American linemen who were as different as night and day. Kenny Dill, a center and linebacker, took so much aggressiveness on the field that he became a menace. We had to watch that boy closely in practice. Once in combat, he turned to fury. Off the field, Kenny, a 6-4 stringbean, was a mild-mannered gentleman.

I remember going down to his hometown, West Point, and telling a civic club: "Kenny is a great player but he's going to cost us a lot of 15-yard penalties."

Big Jim Dunaway, at 6-5 and 265, was just the opposite kind of kid. We had to spend a lot of time firing him up. Or trying to. Meanness just wasn't in him. But he had the talent to make an excellent pro tackle with Buffalo. In the Tennessee game in 1962 a fan jumped out of the stands in Knoxville and a scuffle started in the end zone. A few players got

involved. After the fight ended, Glynn Griffing asked Dunaway why he didn't help his teammates.

"Shucks," Jim replied, "wasn't anyone bothering me."

Field leadership often makes the difference in a game, and
Ole Miss has had good fortune there. The captains and co-
captains who made it all possible between 1947 and 1970
include: Conerly in 1947, Doug Hamley in 1948, Roland
Dale in 1949, Ken Farragut in 1950, Othar Crawford in
1951, Kline Gilbert in 1952, Ed Beatty in 1953, Jimmy
Patton and Allen Muirhead in 1954, Vaughn Alliston in
1955, game captains in 1956, Jackie Simpson and Gene Hick-
erson in 1957, Milton Crain and Kent Lovelace in 1958, Ken
Kirk and Charlie Flowers in 1959, Jake Gibbs and Warner
Alford in 1960, Doug Elmore, Billy Ray Jones and Ralph
Smith in 1961, Glynn Griffing and Louis Guy in 1962, Kenny
Dill and Whaley Hall in 1963, Bobby Robinson and Allen
Brown in 1964, Mike Dennis and Stan Hindman in 1965, Doug
Cunningham and Chuck Hinton in 1966, Michel Haik and Dan
Sartin in 1967, Hank Shows and Robert Bailey in 1968, Glenn
Cannon and Bo Bowen in 1969, and Archie Manning and
Dennis Coleman in 1970.

Since 1961 Ole Miss has considered Jackson, the state capital, its second home. It was in 1961 that Ole Miss dedicated
the new 46,000-seat Mississippi Memorial Stadium there with
a 16-0 win over Arkansas in a nationally televised game.
Lance Alworth, the Mississippi boy we had lost because of
marriage, played halfback for the Porkers.

Doug Elmore quarterbacked for us that year, with Griffing
as his back up. Ole Miss scored 326 points, only three less
than the 1959 team. Johnny Cain signed Elmore out of Re-
form, Alabama, which is just east of Columbus near the
Mississippi line. In high school, Doug was a 160-pound fullback. But he was six feet tall and he built his weight up to
almost 190 pounds. Doug was not as tricky as Gibbs with the
football, but he was stronger and his passing was almost as
good. Doug put on quite a show against Arkansas, which was
playing us for the last time in a regularly scheduled game.

In its October 2, 1961, edition, *Sports Illustrated* quoted Coach Broyles of Arkansas as saying:

> I don't like to say this but that field goal last year had very little to do with our discontinuing the series after this year. Mississippi is just too big and too deep and too rough. They wear you out and leave you in bad shape for your conference games.

I wish we could have kept Arkansas on our schedule. There was a lot of regional interest in it. Ole Miss would like to play more intersectional games. Tad Smith dickered from time to time with athletic directors in the Big 10, but he wasn't able to get us a game in that good football area. It doesn't apply anymore, but in the past we had a hard time lining up six SEC games each year.

It has been written that I never got excited on the sidelines, that I was an unruffled man in a brown or green suit hiding his features under a brown fedora. Well, that's the way I wanted it to appear.

A good football team must have poise out there on the field, and it helps when the coach keeps his poise on the sidelines. I'm lucky about outward appearance, I guess. Actually, my insides got tied up in knots. I got nervous before every game. I could tell whether Ole Miss was going to win or lose by the boys' attitudes. Football wasn't a fun situation for me during the 60 minutes of a game. It was an agony that I learned to live with. I hid my doubts.

I think the poise that Ole Miss teams have developed through the years is their biggest asset out on the field. Somehow, in the face of adversity, my Rebels seemed to reach into a reservoir fashioned by pride and come back. I've seen them do it many times. Boys like that make coaching worthwhile.

It takes extra effort and desire to stand above the pack in college football, and nineteen Ole Miss players have earned first-team All-America honors since 1947. That's something we're all proud of. The list includes Charles Conerly, halfback, 1947; Barney Poole, end, 1947-48; Kline Gilbert, tackle, 1952; Crawford Mims, guard, 1953; Rex Boggan, tackle, 1954; Jackie Simpson, guard, 1957; Charles Flowers, fullback, 1959; Marvin Terrell, guard, 1959; Jake Gibbs, quarterback, 1960; Billy Ray Adams, fullback, 1961; Jim Dunaway, tackle, 1962, Glynn Griffing, quarterback, 1962, Kenny Dill, center, 1963; Whaley Hall, tackle, 1963; Allen Brown, end, 1964; Stan Hindman, guard, 1965; and Bill Clay, defensive halfback, 1965; and Glenn Cannon, safety, and Archie Manning, quarterback, in 1969.

I don't want to leave the impression that there is some sort of corollary between All-Americans and Miss Americas, but in 1959 and 1960—when Ole Miss had some of its finest players and teams—two of our prettiest coeds, Mary Ann Mobley and Lynda Lee Mead, were back-to-back Miss Americas. Some comedian said my redshirt policy for football players had been extended to beauty contests. Ah, success.

14

Football Saves A School

College football makes a significant contribution to our American way of life, something it has been doing since 1869 when Rutgers and Princeton met in the first game. I saw its value in 1962 as few coaches have. That year, Ole Miss football had its finest hour and made discipline and honor a landmark in days of agony and violence. I think one of the enduring salutes to college football came in a newspaper headline that appeared far from the sports pages. It read:

CHEERING FOOTBALL CROWD
PUSHES RACIAL STRIFE ASIDE

The story beneath the headline was a national one, and it was written by Relman Morin for the Associated Press on Saturday night, October 6, 1962, under a Jackson, Mississippi, dateline. Morin, a Pulitzer Prize winning reporter, wrote this in his first sentence: "College football temporarily dulled the anguish of racial strife in Mississippi Saturday."

Only six days earlier, Ole Miss students—joined by hundreds of outsiders—had rioted against the enrollment of a black student. Down in his story, Morin said:

> Lest there be any doubt about the feelings of the people who saw the game, another explosion of cheers rang out when it was announced that Michigan had defeated Army, 17-0—although Ole Miss doesn't play either one of them.
>
> "Ole Miss had been fighting the Army all week," a spectator said.
>
> The Houston-Ole Miss game was played in Jackson, rather than at the Oxford campus, because Federal authorities felt the danger of further disturbances was too great. As students arrived, they looked like any other college crowd—in fact, better behaved than some. It was Joe College with Betty Coed on his arm, out to cheer his team to victory. The Rebels obliged, crushing Houston 40-7.

Morin's keen insight was on the right track, but, as it turned out, the Ole Miss football team did more than temporarily dull the anguish. I am convinced that successful football kept Ole Miss from closing its doors that year. The role of James Meredith, a black Mississippian who integrated the University of Mississippi, has been added to the pages of our nation's history. But I feel the story of what happened to my football team and its part in the crisis has been overlooked. I owe it to a courageous bunch of boys to tell of their deeds. Their accomplishments rate a chapter in the history of collegiate football.

The entire 1962 season remains in my mind quite vividly. The record book shows that Ole Miss finished in third place in all the national polls with this fine 9-0 mark:

September 22	Memphis State	21-7
September 29	Kentucky	14-0
October 6	Houston	40-7
October 20	Tulane	21-0
October 27	Vanderbilt	35-0
November 3	LSU	15-7
November 10	Chattanooga	52-7
November 17	Tennessee	19-6
December 1	Mississippi State	13-6

More than football was at stake in 1962. A terrible thunderhead had built up in our state that summer over the possible entry of James Meredith into Ole Miss. It began on January 26, 1961, when the registrar at the university received an application for admission from Meredith. His application was turned down, and on May 31, 1961, Meredith filed a suit in the United States District Court for the Southern District of Mississippi, seeking an injunction. The case remained in the courts until September 10, 1962, when U. S. Supreme Court Justice Hugo Black of Alabama issued an injunction against any interference with the judgment and mandate of the Fifth Circuit Court of Appeals in New Orleans, which found that Meredith had been denied admission to the university because he was a Negro. No further legal avenue was available to the state, a fact that set President John F. Kennedy and Governor Ross Barnett on a collision course. The President was determined to back court mandates and enroll Meredith; Barnett was determined to keep him out. Something had to give.

Despite the onrushing showdown in the crisis, I opened fall drills on September 1, trying to keep a business as usual attitude. The boys worked hard and on September 22 we went up to Memphis and whipped one of Coach Billy Murphy's strong Memphis State teams, 21 to 7. Meanwhile, the integration situation deteriorated. Newspapers, radio and television took the story to the nation as the State Board of Trustees, caught between federal and state injunctions, turned its powers over to Governor Barnett. He personally appeared on the campus September 20 and rejected Meredith's application. United States marshals escorted Meredith to and from the campus. Ten days later President Kennedy issued Proclamation No. 3497, commanding the governor and others to "cease and desist" obstructing Federal court orders. Later in the same day President Kennedy issued Executive Order No. 11053, which said the Proclamation had not been obeyed. An awful night in Ole Miss history was about to occur.

The explosiveness of the situation hit me on Saturday, September 29, when we played Kentucky in a night game in Jackson. I never saw a more emotional setting. Making a late entrance, Governor Barnett elicited a mighty roar from the crowd. Confederate flags waved everywhere, backing Barnett in his defiance of federal court integration orders. On the field my boys methodically whipped the Wildcats, 14 to 0. If the excitement of the game did not match that of the crowd, it was just as well.

As darkness fell the next day I was in my office on the campus studying films. My staff and I were getting ready for the University of Houston, our Homecoming Day opponent on Saturday, October 6. I had no idea that President Kennedy had made a dramatic television appeal for calm on the campus. When I came out of the film room about 7 p.m. someone—I think it was a security man—entered the athletic building and told me federal marshals had brought Meredith onto the campus. The officer said a yelling mob had gathered at the Lyceum, and asked me to go to the scene to see if I could do anything about controlling the students.

I immediately went up to the Lyceum, which was ringed with U. S. marshals. I walked out into the mob, but I didn't stay long. Everyone was shouting and throwing anything he could pick up. The area in front of the Lyceum, known as the Grove because of its giant oaks, grew more hostile by the minute. I never saw anyone out there I knew. A lot of them weren't students. Gerald Gaia, a student from Memphis, said Buck Randall, a fullback on my team, had argued with the crowd before I got there, telling students he knew to go back to their dorms. I realized Ole Miss was caught in a terrible drama, but I had no idea that 20,000 Army troops—Task Forces Alpha and Bravo—under the command of General Creighton Abrams would be converging on Oxford within hours. Before the night was over, two young men, Paul I. Guihard of Agence France-Presse, a newsman, and Walter Ray Gunter, a jukebox repairman from nearby Abbeville, were shot to death on our campus and nearly 300 other persons were injured.

Worried about my players, I left the Lyceum area and went to Miller Hall to talk to them. I told the boys to stay inside and ordered the doors locked so no one could come in. The boys stayed put. "There was a lot of noise as the riot grew," Glynn Griffing told me. "Some tear gas seeped into the building, but we stuffed towels around the windows to keep it out."

Troops reached the campus just after midnight. Captain Murry C. Falkner, a nephew of the novelist, led the first unit to arrive—Troop E, 2d Reconnaissance Squadron of the 108th Armored Cavalry Regiment. The captain and his men—Mississippi National Guardsmen—came to the rescue of the marshals with four Jeeps and three trucks. In his report to military authorities, Captain Falkner wrote:

> It appeared the Grove was full of people and the street on which we were to drive was a sea of people. The only lights were at the Lyceum and the glow from a burning automobile.
>
> As we passed the Geology Building and the Confederate Statue, a 2x6 piece of lumber was thrown at my Jeep. Fortunately, it missed its target! From there to the Lyceum Building was absolute hell! People would not move out of the street. They threw bricks, concrete, everything and anything they could find—including words. I leaned over to my driver and screamed for him to put the Jeep in second gear and not to slow down or stop for anything.
>
> While we were approaching the Lyceum, one of the men stuck his head out of the back of the truck he was in and started yelling the famous Ole Miss yell, 'Hoddy Toddy.' He didn't get to finish the yell for fear of being 'finished' himself by bricks raining against the side of the truck and into the back.
>
> A person loose in that mob, wearing a uniform, would have been dead.

Early the next morning, around 7 o'clock, I went back into the area. It wasn't easy. There were military roadblocks everywhere. I lived on the campus then, but if you left the area you had a hard time getting back on. Soldiers policed it carefully. I finally got to Miller Hall and found that the boys were all safe. Then I went up around the Student Union Building and the Lyceum. I have never seen such a sight in my life—nothing like it. Right around the Lyceum there were—well, there is no way of estimating, but it looked to me like 5,000 cans of tear gas had been used. The campus resembled a trash dump. It was the worst thing I ever saw. It didn't look like a college campus at all.

How could any of us keep our minds on football? Well, the 1962 team had courage. I have never seen another bunch of boys respond so well to my requests. They kept their emotions in check. They conducted themselves as gentlemen. In squad meetings, they pledged themselves to keeping things going.

As we began preparations for the Houston game, none of us could have guessed at the ordeal ahead. By midweek, helicopters were landing on our practice fields. Army tents went up at second base on the baseball diamond. We had to move our practices into Hemingway Stadium. There were articles in newspapers saying that Ole Miss had put up its usual "Secret Practice" sign. It was a joke. Each day when we worked out there were a couple of thousand troops standing around watching us. Frankly, I think we were quite lucky to have a place to work. I watched many touch pass football games by Army boys.

Ole Miss faced six crucial days after the Sunday night riot. The life of the university was at stake. Mississippians were divided on the question, but I felt the vast majority shuddered at the idea of closing down. William B. Street, political editor of *The Commercial Appeal* in Memphis and a former Ole Miss student, wrote:

> One side urged the Governor to make his stand, maintain his principles and tell the people he would do everything in his power to keep the University of Mississippi and other institutions segregated.
>
> The others called for the 'go to jail' pledge and urged the flat promise that no institution would be integrated as long as 'I am Governor.' Both sets of advisers included members of the Citizens Council, but those who counseled caution faced a risk of being labeled integrationists. . .
>
> There were those who wanted the Governor to close the university as a last resort to prevent Meredith's entry and others who pointed out it would mean sacrificing 5,000 white students for one Negro. They managed to make this point with the Governor.

The enrollment of Meredith did not end our troubles. Early one night I got a telephone call from the White House. It was the attorney general, Robert Kennedy.

"Coach Vaught," he said, "I want you to do what you can to keep the situation calm."

I said I would, but by Tuesday our Homecoming game with Houston had become a pawn between state and federal forces, between the Justice Department and the Army. Nicholas Katzenbach, the assistant attorney general, was on the campus and talked to me several times. It took a tremendous fight to keep the game with Houston from being cancelled. I felt it essential that the game be played, that it might be the key to getting the campus to settle down. I was told that General Hamilton Howze, the senior Army man on the scene, wanted the game played on campus as scheduled. The Justice Department said no.

On October 3, a report by Neal Gregory in *The Commercial Appeal* said:

> The University reconfirmed its decision to carry on normal Homecoming activities at Ole Miss, including the game with the University of Houston after more conferences with military and Justice Department officials. United States Assistant Attorney General Nicholas Katzenbach told a news conference: 'Meredith has plans which will take him off the campus, irrespective of whether the game is played or not.'

I told the squad the game would be played in Hemingway Stadium, but Wednesday night—just three days before the game—Katzenbach and Edwin Guthman, a Justice Department public information officer, flew to Washington. They discussed the site of the game and other aspects of the crisis with the attorney general. A decision against a campus game was made in Washington. I told the boys the game had been shifted to Houston and we would fly down there.

Meanwhile, everything rode a see-saw. For the first time in my life I began to think about how Americans really feel about freedom—about things that people could do and the government couldn't do. Events at Ole Miss made me realize that government—state and national—could do what it wanted to do. The situation at Ole Miss in 1962 was the worst thing I have ever been through. After much maneuvering by Chancellor Williams and Tad Smith, the Justice Department and the Army agreed to let the Homecoming game be played in Jackson. Somehow, all of us kept our sanity. Caught in a highly emotional tug of war, the university teetered close to destruction. A radical minority screamed for the chancellor's scalp, but he and concerned alumni worked to keep the doors open. Many students appealed to their parents to back the chancellor. Our football team helped to tip the scales. I don't think there is any doubt about it. As Morin detected in his Jackson dispatch, football helped to ease tension throughout the state.

As my boys know, I am not a Knute Rockne in the dressing room. My remarks to the team just before the Houston game were brief. I put it to them simply: "It is very important that we play this game, boys, and we have to win it." Boys became men that night. I felt chill bumps as the team let out a roar and swept out of the dressing room at Memorial Stadium in Jackson. The boys whipped Houston, 40 to 7, and I think then and there they sensed that no one would be able to stop them, that a university rode on their shoulder pads.

Tulane fell, 21 to 0 and Vanderbilt lost, 35 to 0. As usual, one of the major hurdles for us was Louisiana State University and its famed Tiger pit in Baton Rouge. Two nights before the game, Ole Miss students staged a big pep rally at the Student Union Building, about two city blocks from Miller Hall. Our football successes had aided in a return to normalcy, but the Army and the Justice Department were nervous, understandably perhaps, over what might happen when that many students gathered in one place and in a doubly charged atmosphere.

Soldiers stood watch at the rally. At the conclusion, several hundred students broke and ran toward Miller Hall. A somewhat similar route would take them to Baxter Hall, where Meredith stayed. Soldiers watched apprehensively. One of them nervously adjusted his mask and got his gas gun to the ready. The students didn't even notice. They charged past the guards and on to Miller Hall, where they cheered the football team for 30 minutes. It was the healthiest sign since the September 30 nightmare. The minds of the students were off campus troubles and on football. Later, a student told me he hadn't noticed the Army men as he ran. The team, with Griffing and Louis Guy as co-captains, went to Baton Rouge and whipped LSU, 15 to 7. The game was easier than the score.

The 1962 team had quality. We used the Winged T offense with a wingback in motion. Griffing, our senior quarterback, had fine rhythm. He could throw the ball and he could run our 45-degree sprint out with power. Three speedsters, Dave Jennings, Chuck Morris and Louis Guy, hit the quick slants and swept the flanks. Perry Lee Dunn and Buck Randall provided the power at fullback.

Up front, we had what Southeastern Conference writers often refer to as a "typical Ole Miss line"—big, tall and fast. There was big Jim Dunaway. He wore a size 15 shoe and he weighed at least 265 pounds, but he could outrun some of our ends for 15 yards. Dunaway made some of our other big men, such as Billy Carl Irwin (6-5 and 200), look small. The tackle opposite Dunaway—Jim Roberts—weighed 245 pounds. The team had athletes on it. Other names like Don Dickson, Richard Ross, Kenny Dill, Bob Upchurch, Larry Smith, Whaley Hall, Joe Dean, Cecil Ford, Bo Aldridge, Rodney Mattina, Wes Sullivan, Bobby Robinson, Tommy Lucas, Don Windham, Fred Roberts, Allen Brown, Woody Dabbs, Reed Davis and Frank Kinard Jr. come to mind.

By the end of November campus life appeared to be normal, except for a few troops here and there. But my troubles were not over. Some of my players, including Griffing, got involved in some off-campus rowdyism that had nothing to do with integration.

Glynn and a carload of his friends drove up to Holly Springs, a few miles north of Oxford, and bought a few cans of beer. While they were parked on the side of the road, another auto filled with boys drove up and a row started. I learned about the incident when Burns Tatum, chief of campus security, came up to me and said:

"You've got to kick Griffing out of school."

I called Glynn in and asked him about the fight, in which one kid had been hurt. Griffing admitted that he had driven to Holly Springs, but said he had not gotten out of the car when the other vehicle drove up and threw a spotlight on them. I asked him who had. "Coach," he replied, "I can't tell you." I learned he had told the truth about himself. But the seniors, including Griffing, who won All-America honors along with Dunaway that year, called a squad meeting. Restrictions were imposed for the rest of the season. The togetherness welded from the integration strife held. During the next four weeks Chattanooga, Tennessee, and Mississippi State would lose to us. In the Tennessee game, which we won 19 to 6, Guy staved off a Vol threat deep in our territory. He intercepted a pass thrown by Mallon Faircloth and ran it back 103 yards for a touchdown. That run got to me. When Louis came off the field I remember grabbing him and saying, "God bless you, son."

To be honest about it, Mississippi State came awfully close to ruining our perfect season. Late in the game, Jimmy Weatherly, our sophomore quarterback, missed a handoff to tailback Dave Jennings on a quick slant into the line. Thinking quickly, Weatherly stuck the ball on his hip and took off running around the right side in a classic bootleg play. He made it all the way, and that gave us the game, 13-6.

Traditionally, the winner of the Ole Miss-Mississippi State football game wins a trophy known as the Golden Egg. *The Commercial Appeal* gave the inside story of the game with a report under this headline:

THE GOOF THAT LAID THE GOLDEN EGG

Indeed, there had been a miscue. But if that's what it takes to have a perfect season, win a conference championship and go to a major bowl I'll buy. I like to think though, that the final game of the season and the newspaper account indicate something more important had happened at Ole Miss. A nightmare had ended. When Ole Miss needed to survive and build a new image, as it sorely did in 1962, a great football team stepped forward.

I always will rate the 1962 team as one of the most courageous in the history of the game. And I agree with a speech Chancellor Williams made in Greenville after calm returned to the campus. He said:

> Riot, lawlessness, destruction, murder—that is the image of the university and of Mississippi that has been given to the world by television, by radio, by newspaper, by every media of communication that exists in this era of Telstar and moonshots. I will not try to brighten that picture. But I will say to you here and now that this is not the whole picture. If it were the whole picture, I would not be speaking to you here today.

Chancellor Williams' personal struggle to save Ole Miss is part of the missing picture. So is college football, the vehicle that gave Mississippi something to cheer.

15

"Mississippi Mules"

When an old gray mule showed up on our campus on Monday, November 10, 1969, the news bureau at Ole Miss got a picture and started processing it to send out on United Press International's Telephoto network.

But it never moved on the wires. Billy Gates, our sports publicity director, heard about it and talked the news bureau out of it. Gates hollered because it was the week of the Tennessee game and the mule bore this sign on its left rump: "Squeeze the Orange."

A coach must be honest with newsmen. He is a public figure and represents a university, but he would be a fool if he told reporters everything he knew—or thought he knew—about opposing teams. That would be like handing your scouting report to the other coach. But I will say this—mules can kick. A man doesn't have to be a country boy or a football coach to know that. The point is this: football is a psychological game.

My staff and I were constantly on the alert for some item, some tidbit that would help us prepare for a game. Ole Miss has won many games, some of them mighty big ones, by entering them with a psychological edge. I have been accused of being too tightlipped about Ole Miss. Perhaps that is a fair appraisal, but my approach was not without reason. I can live with the charge.

I instructed my players to be most careful of what they say to newsmen. Flushed and perhaps angry from a scrap just ended, they might blurt out something that will hurt you later. But I allowed interviews, hoping that the boys' good judgment would see us all through.

In my office I kept a special folder that was nothing more than a psychological file on every team Ole Miss played since I became coach in 1947. It paid rich dividends.

Our game with Tennessee on November 15, 1969, in Jackson puts everything I've been saying into a neat package. Coming into that crucial game with us, Coach Doug Dickey's Volunteers were unbeaten and untied. Tennessee ranked third in the nation. The days built up with that special tension. You could taste it, feel it. There was a heady, dizzy wind of excitement stirring Mississippi from the Gulf to Memphis, and we were all swept up in it.

Ole Miss had taken two conference losses, one an unforgivable 10-9 setback at Kentucky and the other a 33-32 decision at Alabama in what was called by ABC sportscasters Chris Schenkel and Bud Wilkinson the most exciting game telecast by the network in 1969.

But let's back up a year. The first blow of the Mississippi-Tennessee game was not struck in Jackson. It took place a year earlier in Knoxville. My quarterback, Archie Manning, a sophomore, had a bad day in Neyland Stadium in 1968. Tennessee intercepted five of his passes and whipped us soundly, 31 to 0. In the dressing room after the game, Tennessee's fine linebacker, Steve Kiner, made this statement: "It's not so tough defending against Manning. He'll tell you what he is going to do with his eyes. He looks where he's going to throw or send a runner."

This didn't set too well with Archie. He worked from that

day on with an eye on Tennessee. He also worked long hours breaking the habit of telegraphing his plays. A good sophomore learns.

Kiner delivered the second lick in the 1969 game also. It came in August when newspapers which cover the activities of the SEC send reporters around to visit with coaches and players, using a chartered airplane to shorten travel time. They call this group Skywriters.

The tour reached Tennessee and during a break in the usual question and answer routine, Kiner remarked that he had heard the Skywriters had selected Ole Miss as the SEC favorite.

"I hear you guys think Ole Miss has all the horses this season," Kiner said. "Well, the way I see it, all they've got down there is mules."

Kiner's observations in 1968 and 1969 went into my file. I couldn't have done better if I had written them out for him. I understand that Bob Woodruff, Tennessee's athletic director, tried to get Kiner to retract his statement about the mules. He refused, and the issue remained. Sports cartoonists got into the act. Mississippians said they would "hee haw" at Kiner each time Ole Miss scored.

In Tennessee, big orange-colored "Archie Who?" buttons appeared. Perhaps Gates acted properly in getting excited about that old gray mule the students stationed on our campus. But the biggest thing, to my mind, was the reference to Archie's eyes that I had filed a year earlier. When our buses headed toward Jackson I knew we had an edge.

College football players play the game much better today than in the past. They're bigger and smarter and the football they play approaches applied science. Nothing, absolutely nothing, is left to chance. The human element remains, of course, and the game will never become dull and purely mechanical.

But a football coach, especially if he's been around 25 or more seasons and has started casting a wary eye on convalescent homes, lives for the perfectly executed game, one where the boys put all the pieces together in that big puzzle. I've had only one or two games that even came close to fitting a scientific mold, but the Ole Miss-Tennessee game in 1969 certainly must be one of them.

Tennessee had an Orange Bowl invitation in its pocket if it could whip us. Oddsmakers said Ole Miss would lose by a touchdown or more. But my boys had started to click. We had whipped Vince Dooley's Georgia squad and a fine LSU team that Coach Charlie McClendon had put together.

Our lights burned every night getting ready for Tennessee. In our film rooms—one for offense, one for defense—the boys studied as hard as they have ever studied an opponent. The staff forgot about sleep.

Eddie Crawford, scouting Tennessee, had done everything but sleep with the Vols during their march to a 7-0 record. Eddie was in Knoxville when Tennessee beat South Carolina, 29-14, the Saturday before they were to meet us. He caught a plane out of Knoxville right after the game and arrived in Oxford that night.

Except for time off for church, the staff worked through Sunday. By Monday night I could feel that progress had been achieved. In addition to our film study, we had put everything into the computer. It told us exactly what Tennessee had done and where. We knew the plays Coach Dickey's boys counted on and in what field position and the down. We knew exactly what they had done offensively from every situation. Every pass route Tennessee had run was charted.

Of course, you never know what a team might do differently, but you have got to stop what it likes to do. We realized, too, that we would have to have tremendous individual efforts from our boys.

My staff agreed that to win our defense would have to do the job. Tennessee had proven it could score. Its offense had scored points at a clip of 31, 45, 55, 26, 41, 17 and 29 coming up to us. Its quarterback, Bobby Scott, was effective, and Coach Dickey had produced a powerful runner in fullback Curt Watson. The defense was typical Tennessee—tough enough to get the job done. The most points it had given up in a game were 19, those to Auburn while winning by 26. Their front line had size and their linebackers, Kiner and Jack Reynolds, were All-Americans. In fact, the more I looked at the Vols the more I became convinced that their defense was as good as any I had seen at Tennessee.

I did not think Ole Miss strong enough to mount a consistent offense against them, although I knew they were limping in a couple of spots. All of our intelligence told us that Tennessee would be setting its defenses to stop Manning from sprinting out wide. Thus, we decided to go inside.

Coach Dickey, now coaching at the University of Florida, said, "Yes, we moved to stop the outside threat and to take away the short passes. We weren't too concerned with the short running game."

You can see the collision course. In Knoxville, Coach Dickey's staff worked to stop our conventional sprint-out attack. In Oxford, we drilled to rip at the belly until it hurt enough to force Tennessee to move more people inside.

It's like the supply and demand theory in economics. The more demand we could put on Tennessee's supply the better were our chances. We also decided to go with something we hadn't used all season. We call it a quickie, a little running play right at the middle of the defensive line. Tennessee used a four-man front, so we could trap the first inside man—to either side of the center—depending on which way we slanted the play.

Archie Manning made simple handoffs to a running back and we discovered that it worked tremendously well, especially off the I-formation. It worked on the first series. The quickie promptly led us to the play that broke the game open. It came on the eighth play from scrimmage. Ole Miss had a first down on the Tennessee 41 when Archie stopped his handoffs. Moving effortlessly to his right, he threw to Floyd Franks, our flanker, who had found the Tennessee secondary frozen in confusion. Franks caught the ball at the 13 and ran down to the three. Archie, his eyes looking right at Kiner, pushed it across on the third try. The game was four minutes and 29 seconds old.

Tennessee had been off balance since the start, I could see that. But could Ole Miss stop them? From films, scouting and the computer, we had decided that a 54 Call would be the best general defense. That means we used a five-man front and the secondary called its position after the Tennessee offense came to the line. Glenn Cannon, our safety, made the calls.

A checklist, which my secretary put to press each Thursday, noted our best pass defense (Stone Dan against Tennessee; Dan is our jargon for diamond) as well as the best run defense. I kept a copy of the checklist in my coat pocket on the sidelines. In the Tennessee game, the coaches in the press box—Kinard, Dale, Crawford and Tyler—had the same data.

As it turned out, our first general defensive plan proved to be right. Coach Poole's defensive front was ready. Curt Watson tried his favorite power run to the right and was stacked up. Scott, on third down and needing five, went to his favorite receiver, Ken Delong. We knew he would. Our defensive backs were there to break it up. On fourth down, we put a hard rush on the nation's No. 2 punter, Herman Weaver, and he kicked weakly, turning the ball over to us on the Tennessee 37.

Tennessee had taken the ball on the kickoff after our score at its 14, and there we were with the ball just 23 yards up the field. It seemed unbelievable. I thought of what Kentucky coach Johnny Ray had said when he was asked how he thought the game might be won: "A big play will win it, maybe even helped out by a bad punt."

This, then, was the time to stick it to Tennessee. Manning did. We led 13-0 with 5:38 left in the opening quarter. Our defense worked; our offense worked. We were on our way—to the Sugar Bowl to beat No. 2 ranked Arkansas and gain national recognition. Across the stadium grass, the Tennessee staff knew the game was over too. In an interview with Kyle Griffin, sports editor of *The Commercial Appeal*, Coach Dickey reviewed the game after he moved to his new post in

Florida. I was surprised to learn that we agreed on the factors leading to victory and defeat. Doug told Kyle:

> We knew we had to stop the outside game that Ole Miss would have to use in order to hurt us badly and quickly. So I decided to play against the short passes, to try and take them away from Manning.
>
> To accomplish this, I had each man coming out picked up first by a short man and then, if he went on by on a deep pattern, another safety would come up to play him. But Ole Miss came at us in what should have been our most secure area—the middle. Of course, Kiner was injured but still they made that running game click.
>
> When it came time for Manning to really test us—to try to beat us at what we had worked hardest on—we suddenly looked like children out there.
>
> Franks came out and then turned and ran right through the gap between the short defenders. Our deep safety, who was filling in for Bill Young, just stood there, apparently watching for more plays in the middle. There wasn't anyone within 10 yards of Franks when Manning unloaded.
>
> That is the play that beat us. They knew then they could at least try anything they wanted to and have a good chance of it working. We were hurt with Kiner and Young and I don't know if Ole Miss knew this or not, but they sure played like they did.
>
> I could see at the outset that Kiner was going to be of no use to us whatsoever. But he wanted so badly to play. He, too, was concerned over what he had said and all that had been made of it. Once he was in there, what could I do? If I had pulled him out, the whole place would have fallen in. I made a mistake in starting him. And he wouldn't help me out at all. He was too tough to give up and go down or come out on his own.
>
> Kiner wasn't the only thing. Never in all my years of coaching did I have such a day as that one. They seemed to know our very thoughts. Never did I think all my chickens would come home to roost in such a manner. And I hope they never do again.

The game ended, 38-0. I understand how Doug felt. I still remember that 47-0 pasting I took from Bear Bryant and Babe Parilli in 1949.

At the half, I always sit with the quarterbacks and discuss

the things we have done and the things we need to do. In the Tennessee game we were ahead, 24-0, and well, there was not much change necessary. In fact, we did nothing. We stayed with our game plan. I remember Archie kept wanting to put the ball in the air more. I think he wanted to do that mainly because of Kiner. But I told him things were moving along just fine.

"Archie," I said, "let's don't change anything."

I try not to get too emotional after a game, but when we went to the dressing room after whipping Tennessee—which went on to win the SEC championship—I told the squad: "I ought to make you a speech, boys. This is the greatest team effort I've ever seen. When you get my age you'll know how I feel."

Then I sat down. If I hadn't I would have fallen.

16

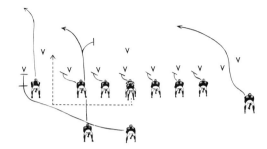

Other Memorable
Games

Trying to sort out memorable games over a span of 25 seasons is a little like asking a man to name his favorite son. But one that stands out in my mind happened on October 31, 1959–a Halloween night–the night that Billy Cannon took a Gibbs punt and ran 89 yards to whip Ole Miss, 7-3.

Outside of the Louisiana Purchase in 1803, many Cajuns consider that run the greatest event in the state's history. Ticket stubs from that famous game–Louisiana State ranked first in the nation, Ole Miss second–have been kept as souvenirs. Newspaper clippings about the game remain in family Bibles.

Radio tapes of Cannon's run may still be obtained. I listened to one as I began writing this chapter. The broadcast begins with 10:38 left in the fourth quarter and Ole Miss ahead, 3-0. Here's the LSU announcer's description:

> It's actually about third down. About 19 yards to go. Going back into punt formation is Jake Gibbs. Of Ole Miss. He stands on his

own 28. He gets the pass from center. He boots it—and gets another nice kick away, going way down field.

Billy Cannon watches it bounce.

He takes it on his own 11! Comes back up field to the 15, stumbles momentarily. He's at the 20! He's running hard at the 25. Gets away from one man at the 30. . .still running at 35. . .45. . .He's on the 50. He's in the clear at the 45!. . .40. . .15. . .10. . .5. . .He scores!

Listen to the cheers as Billy Cannon comes off the field. . .Great All-American!

As everyone in Louisiana can tell you, Cannon ran right by me and the Ole Miss bench on that run, surely one of the greatest in the history of collegiate football. That boy could have gone down at least four times, but he simply wouldn't be headed.

Ordinarily, a back doesn't try to field a bouncing ball around his 10-yard line. Cannon didn't intend to field it, but it took a high, crooked bounce right at him. He had to run with it. Our punt coverage was good. Larry Grantham, a sure tackler, was the point man, but the films show he made a mistake. When the ball hit the ground, Larry let up a step. He knew Cannon wouldn't try to play it, but the crazy bounce took care of that. Cannon got by Grantham.

After the game, newsmen crowded around Cannon in the LSU dressing room. One reporter asked Billy what he had to say about that great run. In a classic remark, Cannon said: "Nothing." Nothing could ever be said to add to such an individual achievement.

But the game didn't end there. Ole Miss took the football on the LSU kickoff and drove to the one-foot line with Doug Elmore, a third-string sophomore quarterback, at the controls.

With fourth down on the LSU one, Ole Miss called time out. I sent in a play—35 Slant-keep, a slide to the left by Elmore. LSU, as expected, went into a Gap-8 defense, a routine goal-line stand. Big and strong, Elmore should have scored, but our sophomore center got mixed up. He blocked away from the call and an LSU lineman got a hand on Doug. This allowed Cannon and Warren Rabb to make the tackle.

I've often wondered how sports historians would have treated this game if Elmore had scored. But it was Billy Cannon's night and his run against us, as much as anything, brought him the Heisman Trophy, which he deserved.

Critics say I sat on three points in that game. Bobby Khayat kicked us into the lead midway the first period, but it should be remembered that Ole Miss had to settle for three points. When we started with a first down at the LSU 8, I wanted a touchdown. But the LSU defense stiffened and with third down at the 3, Mickey Mangham broke through and set us back to the five.

Except for Cannon's run, Ole Miss dominated a bruising defensive game. But Billy ran by Grantham, Richard Price, Jerry Daniels and Gibbs, all good tacklers, and the just must get their due. During the game—played on an okra-slick field—LSU fumbled four times and our kicking strategy was wise. Ole Miss kicked a few times on first down that night, but the big run came on a third-and nineteen-situation. That's almost an automatic kick situation on a damp field.

There shouldn't be any second-guessing to detract from this game. Fred Russell of the *Nashville Banner* said it was the best football game he had seen in his 31 years of covering sports. Governor John McKeithen of Louisiana once said that Cannon's punt return and Ole Miss' drive to the goal line was almost too much for a fan to take. If he'll add coaches to his list, I'll agree.

The greatest chase I ever saw in football took place on the same field that Cannon made his run. Actually, the game proved to be less than a barn-burner, but I'll never forget Stan Hindman's rundown of Joe Labruzzo on November 2, 1963. Joe appeared to have a 10-yard lead on Stan, but Hindman cut him off.

David Bloom wrote it this way in *The Commercial Appeal:*

> The frustration of the Bayou Tigers, contained in all phases by the
> best defense in the nation, reached a zenith in the third quarter. Joe

Labruzzo fielded a punt on his 18, stumbled, then ran 81 yards
through the whole Ole Miss team in the wake of superb blocking.
And, of all things, the little 175 pound scatback, was overhauled at
the one by Stan Hindman, a 230 pound Ole Miss lineman. But that's
not all. In four plays from this high point, Louisiana State was
thrown for four losses and surrendered the ball at the five.

The 37-3 score and fullback Fred Roberts' three touchdowns had to take a second row to that sterling play.

Sixty minutes of Southeastern Conference football can
drain players and coaches. The most emotional game—ever—
for me came October 5, 1969, against Alabama in Birmingham. Coach Bryant's boys beat us, 33 to 32, in a game that
left me and the Bear stammering.

"I've never seen a game like it, not with us in it," Bryant
said.

I told newsmen that I had never had a team to put everything it possibly had into one football game, but the boys did
that against Alabama and we were still one point short. ABC
telecaster Chris Schenkel said, "It's the most exciting game
I've ever seen in 20 years of broadcasting."

Millions across the nation saw the game, which ended a few
minutes before midnight. Archie Manning set a fistful of
records; so did his Alabama counterpart, Scott Hunter. Certainly, this was a once-in-a-lifetime game. I call it the record
book game. Archie threw the ball 52 times and completed 33
for 436 yards. He ran 15 times for 104 yards, giving him 540
yards in total offense. Hunter hit 22 of 29 passes for 300
yards and picked up 3 yards in 9 rushes, giving him 303 yards
in total offense. The game rewrote NCAA, Southeastern Conference and school records. Here they are:

NCAA

Two-team, single game offense with most passes completed—
Manning and Hunter, 55. Previous high 53 by New Mexico (37) and
Texas-El Paso (16), 1967; and Brigham Young (32) and Texas-El
Paso (21), 1966.

Southeastern Conference

Pass attempts—Manning 52. Previous high 49 by Florida's Steve Spurrier vs. Miami, 1966.

Pass completions—Manning 33. Previous high 27 by Spurrier vs. Auburn, 1966.

Passing yardage—Manning 436. Previous high 409 by Florida's John Reaves vs. Houston, 1969.

Total Offense—Manning 540. Previous high 414 by Georgia's Larry Rakestraw vs. Miami, 1966.

Team pass attempts—Ole Miss 52. Previous high 51, Florida vs. Miami, 1966.

Team pass completions—Ole Miss 33. Previous high 29 by Ole Miss vs. Chattanooga, 1947.

Team passing yardage—Ole Miss 436. Previous high 407 by Georgia vs. Miami, 1950.

Total offensive plays—Manning 67. Previous high 62 by Manning vs. Southern Mississippi, 1968, and Tennessee's Bubba Wyche vs. Auburn, 1968.

Most passes without interception in a game—Alabama 30. Previous mark 28 by Florida vs. Florida State, 1965.

That fantastic game rewrote eleven Ole Miss and three Alabama team records. One newspaper quoted me as saying, "Archie, Archie. . .what a performance." Perhaps I did. I just don't remember that. I do remember telling the boys at halftime that the game meant more to me than any I had ever coached, and that the view went whether we won or lost. Ironically, the winning Alabama touchdown was scored by George Ranager—from Meridian, Mississippi.

Twice in my career at Ole Miss I have sent in men with impulsive instructions. The last time was October 19, 1968, at Hemingway Stadium. I called Vernon Studdard, a flanker, to my side and said, "Vernon, I want you to catch the ball and score. When you do, bring me the ball."

Chased by the officials, Vernon ran up to me 20 seconds later and put the ball in my hands. At the time, we were tied with Southern Mississippi, 7-7, with 4:49 remaining in the game. We had the ball at the Southern 49 when Vernon took the play in to Archie. Perry King kicked the extra point and Ole Miss was ahead to stay, 14 to 7.

A few minutes later, Danny Hooker intercepted a Tommy Boutwell pass for us and ran it back 69 yards for another touchdown.

Vernon's catch duplicated what happened to Louis Guy in 1962, the first time I ever told a man to catch a touchdown pass and bring the ball to me. I have always liked boys who followed instructions.

There haven't been many 0-0 games by Ole Miss since 1947—only one to be exact—but my boys took part in such an epic defensive struggle with Memphis State on September 21, 1963. Ole Miss went on to an undefeated season but that opening tie was about as exciting as a fan can expect if he likes purely man-for-man combat. Kenny Dill, our senior line-backer, and MSU's John Fred Robilio dueled as fiercely as two men ever did in the middle of a line.

The game ended in a tie, but to paraphrase Bear Bryant, it wasn't like kissing your sister at all.

17

Quarterbacks
I've Known

It may be a few years before another boy comes along with the talent of Archie Manning, but I've learned to expect surprises. Ole Miss has been blessed with good quarterbacks. Athletic ability and intelligence are essential to their success, but through the years I've found that attitude often is the measure of a man. That's why I remember one of those hot September days back in 1968.

The sun burned down as I walked out of Miller Hall with three big quarterbacks. I heard a katydid singing in the grass somewhere off to the south, but my mind was on other things. We had just completed lunch and were headed for my office for a skull session. My mind toyed with a psychological situation as the boys and I approached my new pickup truck—a red Ranchero.

I knew only three men could sit comfortably in the cab. Without saying a word, I walked around the truck and slipped under the driver's wheel. My quarterbacks looked at each other. Then, all three piled into the front seat with me. I tried to hide a smile as I switched on the ignition, but the athletes with me—Archie Manning, Don Farrar and Shug Chumbler—grinned too. I think they suspected I was testing them.

I wanted all my athletes to be front-seaters. If one of those quarterbacks had crawled into the back of my truck he would have volunteered to take a second row, and that's something the quarterbacks I've known at Ole Miss don't do. They'd rather skin a live skunk.

A lot of other quarterbacks—Jim Plunkett of Stanford, Joe Theismann of Notre Dame, Rex Kern of Ohio State, Lynn Dickey of Kansas State and Dan Pastorini of Santa Clara played in 1970, but I'm convinced that Manning had the edge. He could spot a flaw in the enemy defense—and exploit it—quicker than any other boy I've ever coached. In his junior year Archie was changing 30 per cent of his plays at the line. Archie has to be my best quarterback. One word in the scouting summary on Manning by the New Orleans Saints sticks out in my mind: "Cinch" to play in the National Football League. The Saints' card graded Archie this way:

There was a footnote on the two 6s given Manning, point-
ing out there was no way to grade him on quickness in setting
up and determination to stay in the pocket because Ole Miss
used a sprint-out attack. However, Archie was a dropback
passer in high school and he will be able to adapt to the pro
style.

Over the years, the question sportswriters have thrown at
me most is, "Who was your best quarterback?" I answered it
in 1970 just before the Heisman Trophy vote, but I stressed
there were other days and other boys who helped to place
the stepping stones for Archie. It all began with Charley
Conerly, who was a tailback, not a quarterback. Then there's
Jake—Jake Gibbs, who was our quarterback in 1960, a
national championship year. Jake threw and ran very much
like Manning. The difference was that Archie is larger and
more powerful—6-3½ and 205. Just as Archie, Jake had wonderful vision, a physical asset common in all great passers.
Both developed into super-athletes at Ole Miss.

There are interesting parallels involving Jake and Archie.
Our recruiters recognized the athletic abilities of both, but
their talents in high school seemed to be best in sports other
than football. Jake excelled at baseball at Grenada and
Archie in basketball at Drew. I wish I could write that I went
to Drew and signed Archie myself, but that's not the case.
The honor fell to Roy Stinnett, a graduate assistant on the
coaching staff at the time.

Archie was a football sleeper until the annual All-Star high
school football game in Jackson. He didn't start at quarterback but his passing led the north to a stunning 59 to 33 win
over the south. In his freshman season with us, Archie didn't
burn any barns, but in the spring drills before the 1968
season I saw how quickly Archie could read defensives and
come up with an automatic to exploit it.

In the fall of 1968 when touring Southeastern Conference
writers came to the campus, I told them Archie was going to
be one of my best.

"How do you compare him with Joe Namath?" an Alabama writer asked.

I let the question go with the remark that Ole Miss had never played against Namath. I wish I had told them what I really thought—that Manning would break every record Namath ever set.

Archie and I often discussed the publicity he generated. We also talked about the quick money men who came out with songs and buttons. I told him there would come a time when all of this would have a value to him, that it was what people wanted. Being a remarkably stable human being, Archie never coasted after such a buildup. He realized it couldn't walk up to the line of scrimmage and help him execute a play—and that was uppermost in my mind. Archie concentrated on winning, with the team.

I remember my teams by the quarterbacks, and there have been many great ones. In 1961, Fred Russell of the Nashville *Banner* ran these verses in his "Sidelines" column:

Alas!

When Gibbs joined the Yanks
The Conference thanks
Rose up to the height of the sun.
But we're getting no break,
For right behind Jake,
Stand Elmore and Griffing and Dunn.

They're a triple-threat terror,
And this is no error,
How those boys can pass and can run.
How quick the adoption,
Of the sneak and the option,
By Elmore and Griffing and Dunn.

So it seems that again
High Ole Miss will reign
For all the year '61
From the fearsome attacks
Of three fine quarterbacks.
They're Elmore and Griffing and Dunn.

Glynn Griffing could do everything well. He was brilliant on the option pass or run. He was the best I ever saw at making the third down play. I still think he had great potential for the pros. The New York Giants told me he never was ready when they called on him, but I believe he was mishandled.

A powerful runner, Perry Lee Dunn came to us a passer, but he had trouble hitting his receivers. Rumors got out that he had tunnel vision, but that was a lot of bosh. Perry Lee helped us tremendously with his running ability. Doug Elmore directed Ole Miss through a high-scoring 1961 season. Earlier, he came close to winning football immortality as a sophomore in that 1959 Halloween Night game with LSU, as I have indicated. Some student photographer took a picture of Doug seconds after the game ended. It hurts me even today to look at it and see the tears running down Doug's face.

Going back to 1947, Buddy Bowen was my first quarter-back. In the Notre Dame Box we used, Buddy's main job was to block, something that he did exceptionally well. He earned the Jacobs Trophy as the best blocker in the SEC.

Farley Salmon, Bobby Jabour, Rocky Byrd, Jimmy Lear, Eagle Day, John Wallace Blalack, Houston Patton, Raymond Brown, Bobby Franklin, Jimmy Weatherly, Bruce Newell, Jimmy Heidel and others kept the ball moving for Ole Miss until Manning arrived.

The best thing about coaching is seeing a boy develop into a great football player. Eagle Day turned out to be one of my best quarterbacks, but he came to Ole Miss as green as anyone we ever had. In his senior year Eagle outdueled TCU's fabulous Jim Swink in the Cotton Bowl. Great courage marks the best boys. Jimmy Lear came back from a terrible foot injury to become a fine quarterback. I'll always remember his performance against Maryland. It's understandable that I remember my teams by the quarterbacks.

18

On Going Bowling

Coach Ed Walker took Ole Miss to its first bowl game in 1936, playing Catholic University in the Orange Bowl and losing, 20 to 19, although Catholic didn't make a first down in the second half. Twice Ole Miss had men break into the open and head for touchdowns, but on each occasion they slipped on the sandy Miami turf.

Anything can happen in a bowl game, including the first one on January 1, 1902, when Michigan astounded Stanford, 49 to 0, in the Rose Bowl. As I mentioned earlier, it was in 1929 that Roy Riegels made his famed wrong way run in the Rose Bowl. This, of course, is what makes postseason football such a spectacle.

I'll never forget the 1968 Liberty Bowl game. On the first play from scrimmage, Quarterback Al Kincaid of Virginia Tech pulled a trick play. Without a huddle, he picked up the ball and pitched it to Ken Edwards, a tailback who ran 58 yards for a touchdown. The game was 17 seconds old and Ole Miss was behind, 7-0. That little gambit stunned us, but

Archie Manning, quarterbacking his first bowl game, and Steve Hindman combined their passing and running talents and pulled us out, 34 to 17, on a strange day in Memphis.

In 1964 my boys went to New Orleans to play in the Sugar Bowl and it snowed the day before the game. When four inches of snow fall that far south it's wise to prepare for the unexpected. Our opponent was Alabama, and Bear Bryant had the answer to our defense. He sent in Tim Davis to kick four field goals and whip us, 12 to 7.

My first bowl game at Ole Miss came in 1948 at Memphis against my alma mater, TCU. It was called the Delta Bowl, but it was misnamed. It should have been the Frigid Bowl, for I can't remember a colder day. There had been a tornado in the area the night before the New Year's Day game and then everything turned to ice.

TCU took an early 9-0 lead over Charley Conerly and the boys, but the Horned Frog players made the mistake of their lives. They began to ridicule my Rebels, calling them "Mississippi mudhens" and less friendly names. At the half, the team decided it had heard enough. It went back out on that frozen field and cut up TCU, 13 to 9.

In the 1955 Sugar Bowl game Navy brought its "Team of Desire" to New Orleans and scuttled my SEC champions, 21 to 0. To tell the truth, I suspected disaster from the moment I saw George Welsh, the little Middie quarterback, push up his sleeves and go to work. By the end of the fourth quarter I was ready to turn in my V-5 pin. During the regular season Ole Miss had scored 283 points and given up only 47. Southern sports writers predicted my boys would win handily, but after the game one observer said, "You would figure Ole Miss would get high for this game, but they had about as much pep as an old Southerner who sat on his porch waiting for rain to hit the cotton field." It's much too late to offer excuses, but I may have cost the boys their legs. We trained hard at Biloxi but heavy drills in rain and mud probably hurt us. Our poor showing in that game would help us in our next Sugar Bowl outing, a 39 to 7 romp over Texas in 1958. The boys were tired of criticism.

Ole Miss players guard their national record—14 consecutive bowl appearances—jealously. In 1969 when Archie Manning and his teammates had lost three games early in the season they realized they were about to snap a string. They decided to do something about it. People remember what you do last and the 1969 team's big wins over LSU and Tennessee late in the season opened the doors to the Sugar Bowl game with Arkansas.

I have always felt that if a team has done a good job a bowl bid is a reward for the boys. Financially, John Reed Holley, our business manager, reports that Ole Miss' 18 bowl games since 1947 have grossed $2,250,000, a sum that the school has shared with other members of the Southeastern Conference. The games gave us the equivalent of 18 additional spring practices, but the best part about it, of course, has been the telling of the Ole Miss football story.

In my visits to homes in Mississippi I often see portraits of Ole Miss football players painted on inch-thick sugar slabs 9 inches wide and 15 inches deep. Proud families have put them behind glass and consider them heirlooms. The paintings date back to 1952, the year Ole Miss won the first of its eight invitations to play in the Sugar Bowl. A New Orleans artist, J. Phil Preddy, also painted a picture of the Ole Miss Lyceum, using 702 sugar cubes as a canvas. Thousands saw it, and I think this points up the value of bowl games. The goodwill involved goes far beyond the playing field and the cash register.

Our 1948 Delta Bowl game was not televised, but all the others have been. Millions of Americans who have never been close to Hemingway Stadium in Oxford have seen my teams on their television sets. Through the 1970 season, Ole Miss has participated in 29 televised games:

These are the TV teams:

1952	Georgia Tech	(ABC)	1953 Sugar Bowl
1953	Arkansas	(CBS)	Memphis
1954	Navy	(ABC)	1955 Sugar Bowl

1955	TCU	(CBS)	1956 Cotton Bowl
1957	Texas	(NBC)	1958 Sugar Bowl
1958	Florida	(CBS)	1958 Gator Bowl
1959	LSU	(NBC)	1960 Sugar Bowl
1960	Rice	(NBC)	1961 Sugar Bowl
1960	LSU	(ABC)	campus
1961	Arkansas	(ABC)	Jackson
1961	Texas	(CBS)	1962 Cotton Bowl
1962	Arkansas	(NBC)	1963 Sugar Bowl
1963	LSU	(CBS)	Baton Rouge
1963	Alabama	(NBC)	1964 Sugar Bowl
1964	Mississippi State	(NBC)	campus
1964	Tulsa	(CBS)	1964 Bluebonnet Bowl
1965	Tennessee	(NBC)	Memphis
1966	Texas	(ABC)	Bluebonnet Bowl
1967	Alabama	(ABC)	Birmingham
1967	LSU	(ABC)	Jackson
1967	Texas at El Paso	(SN)	Sun Bowl
1968	Georgia	(ABC)	Athens
1968	Virginia Tech	(ABC)	Liberty Bowl
1969	Alabama	(ABC)	Birmingham
1969	LSU	(ABC)	Jackson
1969	Arkansas	(ABC)	1970 Sugar Bowl
1970	Alabama	(ABC)	Jackson
1970	LSU	(ABC)	Baton Rouge
1970	Auburn	(ABC)	1971 Gator Bowl

Bowl games, telecasts and wire service polls joined with newspapers in shaping the national image of Ole Miss football. I think fans everywhere understand my Mississippians better today than they did 20 years ago. In 1950 Coach Denny Myers' Boston College Eagles visited Oxford and lost, 54 to 0, to one of my worst teams, but a surprised Jack Malaney of the old *Boston Post* came up with one of my favorite sentences:

"Little Ole Miss made a little ole mess of Boston College today."

19

"THANKS FELLAS... FROM TH' BOTTOM OF MY TANK..."

On and Off the Field

One of the first assignments I gave myself after becoming a football coach was a study of motivation. I read a dozen or more books on psychology, making notes of the more important theories on group leadership.

When a boy arrives at Ole Miss he must work hard at being a part of the team. He is taught that togetherness and discipline build winning attitudes. At the same time the game has to be fun. Each year I kept an eye out for a clown, a team jester, to keep us from taking ourselves too seriously. Through the years the policy paid off. A laugh is better than a fistfight when competiton for a starting slot is fierce or a game is close.

In 1960 my backs were running through some drills as we got ready for Rice in the Sugar Bowl. I walked around chewing my lips—a habit—until Frank Halbert, a second-string halfback, spoke to me.

"Coach," he said, "my folks want to be in New Orleans when the team arrives. What time are we going to get there?"

The names of the boys on the traveling squad hadn't been

posted, so I asked, "What do you mean, we?" I looked Frankie right in the eye when I said it. He looked right back at me, his eyes as big as saucers.

"Well, coach," he drawled, "you are going too, aren't you?"

I quit biting my lips and burst out laughing, forgetting about Rice for a few minutes. The court jester had done his job, and he made the trip too.

A good mimic, Halbert used to get behind my back and chew his lips, mocking me. During games I had a habit of rubbing my fingers against my lips, especially after a big Ole Miss play. More than once I noticed Halbert walking right beside me, rubbing his fingers against his lips and saying, "Hot damn!"

Our 1970 team had its prankster in Vernon Studdard, a long-haired flanker signed by the New York Jets. I once told Vernon he would end up as a notorious criminal or a millionaire businessman. I mentioned Vernon earlier when talking about the time I ordered him to catch a touchdown pass and bring the ball to me. Once, during a hot practice session, I had a glass with some ice in it. Vernon looked at that ice sloshing with the saddest eyes I've ever seen, and I said, "Vernon, what will you give me for this?"

His eyes lit up instantly. "Coach," he said, "I'll give you three athletic shirts and an autographed football."

I didn't give him the water. I had just learned something about our shrinking supply of athletic shirts.

You can't coach boys successfully unless you have a sense of humor. In 1953 Eagle Day came to football practice immediately after ROTC drills. One afternoon the quarterbacks were working on automatics at the line of scrimmage, and Eagle took his turn. Just as he reached the center he spotted a back out of position. Instead of calling "Check!" Eagle blurted: "As you was!" I laughed so hard I almost hurt myself.

A coach must be firm and fair with his athletes, but I don't believe in starched collars. From time to time my boys got chuckles at my expense. The time I remember best came in 1967 when we went out to El Paso to play the University of Texas-El Paso in the Sun Bowl. The Touchdown Club there invited the team to a luncheon, and my old TCU idol, Mike Brumbelow, now community relations director for the El Paso Natural Gas Company, called me up for an introduction. As I walked toward the microphone, a woman started running toward me yelling, "Johnny, oh Johnny, where are you honey?"

She had a gown on with a low neck that fairly well exposed her, and her hair was all aflutter. I had no idea what was going on. This wild woman had a fistful of papers in her hand and when she got to the speakers' stand she yelled, "You left your notes in my room." I realized then it was a joke, but she grabbed me and started kissing me. Finally, she turned to my team and said, "Boys, the old coach and I had a good time for a while last night. Then he got tired and I spent the rest of the night patting my foot, singing 'Dixie' and waiting for the South to rise again." My players howled as I stood there—a big, embarrassed clown.

There were many tears in Ole Miss' climb to the top, as the years show, but laughter is part of the Mississippi mystique too. The kids think their football can match that of Notre Dame, Ohio State, Nebraska, Southern Cal and Texas, but they can take good-natured kidding about water marks on their legs and small town backgrounds. Panther Burn isn't overpopulated, so why not laugh with the out-of-state visitor who drives through Mississippi from Tennessee to the Gulf Coast and remarks about the number of little towns that have the same name on highway signs: "Resume Speed."

It's another matter when someone knocks Ole Miss football because the woods are full of Doc Varners and old brown hats that show up at football games. But not all good Mississippians were born in the state. The Rockne of the Ole Miss staff is a Yankee born in Rhode Island—Wesley Knight, our trainer. No man ever loved Ole Miss more. Each season Doc gets out a mimeographed message, a pep talk, to the squad. But he doesn't stop there. Often a player, perhaps one who is having to take a second row, will find a little personal note in his locker from Doc. The undefeated, untied 1962 team dedicated the

LSU game to Doc, and I was elated that we won for a grand man.

I had seen real dedication in Wes Knight at Rensselaer Tech when the Navy sent me to Troy, and when I took over as coach at Ole Miss I called Doc and asked him to come down and help me. Doc wasn't all that excited about moving South, but he said he would look the situation over. While he was in Oxford, Colonel David Alexander and his wife asked Doc and me to dinner. It was Doc's first old fashioned southern dinner, and his eyes darted about when they put catfish, hushpuppies and turnip greens on the table. Finally Doc found his voice and spoke up: "I'll eat your catfish and hushpuppies, but not the turnip greens."

Time changes us all. Now Doc grows greens in his garden. Sometimes I think he is an unreconstructed Rebel. So do the boys, who always remember Doc on his birthday. Usually, they give him $100—and throw him in the whirlpool. Once, back in the early 1960's, the boys gave him the money but forgot the ritual. Doc stomped around muttering. Suddenly, the boys remembered. Into the water went Doc.

Off the field, football has brought Schmos and other strangers to my hotel room doors. One such stranger was John H. Vaught, who knocked on my door in New Orleans in 1958. A Texas supporter, he wore a Stetson and other Western clothes. He also had on an orange tie—a Texas color.

"My name is John Vaught," he said, "and I just wanted to meet you. I want to know what your middle initial stands for. Mine is H. too."

I said, "It's Howard."

"Well," he said, grinning, "I just wondered. Mine's Harold." As he left my room John Harold Vaught said he was an Austin florist. That night, after the Sugar Bowl game, he got on a crowded elevator, and everyone started introducing themselves. When he said, "I'm John Vaught," he almost started a commotion. A tall man in a corner of the elevator had spoken up immediately, "You aren't John Vaught." John Harold Vaught immediately began pulling out identification papers. The man questioning his identity was Tom Swayze, my recruiter.

20

Far From
The Crowds

My favorite bear stories involve Paul Bryant of Alabama and a Minnesota bruin.

Paul's adventures with a bear took place in Fordyce, Arkansas, when he wrestled one as a boy and won his nickname. Mine began in June of 1968 in canoe country near Crane Lake in St. Louis County, Minnesota, a stone's throw from Canada's Ontario Province. Anyone who coaches college football for a living never seems to get away from it completely, even for a few days, but I tried. In late spring or early summer I like to pack my hunting and fishing tackle, sack a few groceries with old copies of *Field & Stream* and *True* and head for the woods, and I jumped at the opportunity when L. O. Crosby of Picayune, Mississippi, a lumberman and an Ole Miss alumnus, invited me to join him on a fishing expedition in the Crane Lake area, where incredibly blue lakes and streams are found.

After getting squared away in Crosby's cottage, our party decided to go up a sparkling little stream. We paddled a canoe for a full day before pitching camp for three days of fishing. Our luck was good but an intruder came into our tent area the first night and began knocking things around. Then he began walking in on us in broad daylight, just as if he were one of us instead of a 300 pound bear.

The bear, at first, fed mainly on the throw-away portion of the fish we caught. But at night he would get into our grocery storage, nosing around primarily for the syrup we had for hotcakes. He kept us awake every night. One morning I got my camera out and began taking pictures of the bear, and he ran up a tree.

Around the campfire at night in a Minnesota June our conversation often would turn to Ole Miss football, particularly the game coming up with Bear Bryant's Alabama team in Jackson, Mississippi. Well, that fall my team edged Bear's 10 to 8, and our friends up in Minnesota heard about it, and they couldn't wait for us to get back to Crane Lake in 1969. It seems that our camp-raiding bear had become a pest and a nuisance and game wardens were forced to kill him. When Crosby and I got back up there a dinner for 12 had been arranged. At its conclusion there was a toast to Ole Miss' victory over Alabama and a special presentation to me of a mounted bear's tail. It is one of two treasured trophies in my den. The other is undoubtedly the nation's most unusual paperweight, a gift from Harold Crump of WLAC-TV in Nashville.

Crump, a very good friend and an Ole Miss alumnus who attends all of our football games and who is tremendously happy when we win the big ones, sent it to me late in 1970. He called me after Ole Miss had defeated Alabama in a nationally televised game. Crump told me the paperweight was something that I didn't have and probably had never seen. He indicated it might be illegal to send it through the mail. When Ole Miss went up to Nashville to play Vanderbilt while I was in the hospital, Crump gave the gift to John Reed Holley, our business manager, to bring to me.

It turned out to be a 20-pound bear trap, with jaws on it strong enough to snap a man's leg. It had a plate on it with this inscription: John H. Vaught trapped the Bear October 3, 1970, and the score was 48-23.

I treasure the mementos because you don't whip Bear Bryant very often. I know from past experience.

But let's get back to the woods. In April, after spring practice is over, I like to go to a hideaway that Mr. and Mrs. Mark Ham of Clarksdale, Mississippi, told me about—Jackson Point, an island they lease in the Mississippi River.

Turkey hunting is excellent there. It is a great challenge to be in the woods—to be out there alone, listening to them wake up. It's amazing how quiet the woods are before dawn and how noisy they suddenly get at daylight. To hunt turkeys you have to get up well ahead of daylight. After a cup of coffee and a sweet roll, you get a flashlight and start out. You scout out places turkeys have been, looking for signs of scratching and feathering. The gobblers start their calls about daybreak, while still on the roost. I always move toward the nearest one—just as close as I dare. Then I sit flat on the ground and lean back against a log.

It's a real thrill if you can get to talking to a turkey and fool that rascal into sight. I call them by mouth, with a hen call. You entice the gobbler to come to you, just as in a football trap play. I have had toms fly directly from the roost to me. All except one—one that I call Frank. He has a big mouth, so I named him after my talkative old ball player and friend, Frank Halbert.

Now Frank struts around among a tremendous herd of hens. I've seen him. Once, I had him coming to me, had him worked out of that big flock, but the unexpected—just as in a football upset—shot me down. An airplane picked that moment to fly over that isolated island, and the noise startled Frank away. I'm going to get that turkey next season because his namesake is an Ole Miss heretic—he's an assistant coach at Mississippi State now.

One of my closest hunting and fishing companions was Bob Carrier, the Cornell alumnus who made a fortune in Mississippi and loved Ole Miss football. In the early 1950's,

Bob and I would go up to Canada and fish streams in the Laurentian Mountains. It's beautiful country, and we would get a canoe and a guide and enjoy marvelous fishing. There's nothing like being far back in the North Woods, lying on a bed of balsam boughs at night and listening to a mountain stream talk to itself.

Bob was 30 years older than I but I never had a finer friend. In the last years of his life he decided to leave Barnacre, a game preserve that Grantland Rice, the great sportswriter, and top corporation executives used to visit for quail hunts, and move closer to the campus. I suggested to Bob that he let me buy the land for him to build on. I figured I could get it at a fairer price, and I bought 17 acres on the northwest edge of the Ole Miss campus. Bob then deeded me three acres close by as a homesite.

In his will Bob remembered me, leaving me $15,000 in cash and giving me some splendid Oriental rugs, which are on the floors of my farm home. He also left me his hunting and fishing equipment. Even though he had given Ole Miss more than a million dollars during his life, Bob Carrier's estate in the final probate report at Ripley, Mississippi, on November 16, 1961, revealed a net worth of $6,641,000. His wife, Mrs. Lenore Woolard Carrier, and his son, R. M. Carrier, Jr., a Louisville, Kentucky, industrialist, were the principal beneficiaries. When Mrs. Carrier died their big Georgian-type home went to the university for use as the chancellor's home.

When he told me he planned to move to Oxford, Bob added, "I want to be near my football team." Ole Miss lost a member of the family when Bob Carrier died. I never knew a finer companion or sportsman. Those hunting and fishing trips put new life into me because during the football season I devoted all my energies to that task. I didn't attend banquets or dinners. I even told Johnsie we were not to have company. Golf, which I enjoy despite a 12 handicap, was out. I had a film room in my home and I worked there at nights. Seven days between games never seemed enough.

I tried to spend most of my Friday nights to myself. I read

a lot, but, from time to time, I would call a friend and ask him to come pace the floor with me. One of them was George Bugbee, sports editor of the *Memphis Press-Scimitar* and a former Texan who grew up at San Marcos. On Saturday mornings before games I liked to be alone as long as possible. Some writers said I was aloof, but that was not the case. I was trying to find the last-minute something, the psychological element to bring to the team's attention. Then, win or lose on Saturday, my schedule never changed. I went back home and went to work. At Ole Miss Sunday is a rigorous day, a terrible thing. Except for the morning church break, the staff works all day and into the night. This schedule prevented me from making a television show on Sunday, something TV producers said cost me $100,000 or more. A TV show is an excellent public relations and recruiting vehicle, but I couldn't afford to take time from Sunday's schedule to fly to Jackson or Memphis to tape a show.

I left a Texas farm when I was 15 and I returned to a farm in 1963, buying 160 acres about five miles west of the campus on Highway 6, the road I took into Oxford back in 1946. Johnsie and I built a ranch house on a site she picked on one of the rolling hills, and, from our breakfast table, we look out on fishing ponds and a few head of Angus cattle.

Both of us love the outdoors. Johnsie fishes just about every day, and each morning when the weather is good I saddle my horse, Tina, and ride, looking at the pastures and relaxing. Sometimes I think about the days back at Ingleside when I rode Prince to the little brick school. Life has a way of coming full circle.

Diary of a Season

In 1970 the federal census counted 2,216,912 Mississippians. That same number, with varying degrees of confidence, expected Ole Miss to win the Southeastern Conference football championship just as sure as Nitta Yuma is in Sharkey County. For 25 seasons I had encouraged such confidence across the state, and I didn't dare suggest things could go wrong. But I knew it would be a tremendous chore. The SEC is as tough a football league as any in the nation. An undefeated team is almost a thing of the past.

A decade ago, I could name five schools in the SEC that Ole Miss could whip by just showing up on the field. Coaching genius was not involved in my thinking. I simply had the best athletes, with the emphasis on big, tall linemen and quick backs. Today, no team in the conference can overlook another. Every school seems to get its share of the athletes, and motivation usually is the difference on a given Saturday. I had seen this turn in southern football long before the 1970 season, but I must confess I didn't like the way the fact came back to haunt me in my last campaign as a college coach.

Every old coach dreams of his final season. He wants to go out a big winner. He wants 44 talented young men to add his philosophies and teaching skills to their own drive and ambition—and win. Well, I am no exception. My farewell, I had decided after the 1969 season, would be with my 1970 squad.

Ole Miss had the makings of a fine team. Everyone in the state could hardly wait for play to begin. My staff and I felt the same way, but we knew our work was cut out for us. Every team we faced would be trying to knock us on our tails.

I expected a rewarding year, perhaps the most rewarding of 25 seasons in the little red hills of North Mississippi. My hopes for 1970 revolved around 25 seniors and our superstar, quarterback Archie Manning.

There was no way to keep this team from receiving the most extensive pre-season ballyhoo of all my Rebel squads. In 1947, when I had two All-Americans in Charley Conerly and Barney Poole, I would have labeled such publicity an injustice to the team. My thoughts were the same in 1960 and 1962 when Jake Gibbs and Glynn Griffing were the best quarterbacks in the country.

But all of us change. The publicity and predictions in 1970 added to the challenge. I would be a candidate for the Young County Liars Club in Texas if I didn't say right at the beginning that I thought Ole Miss would take a 9-0 record into its televised December 5, 1970, game with Louisiana State in Baton Rouge..

A nightmare roused me from my dreams. Perhaps I should blame Murphy's Law for what happened to Ole Miss and me, but I have always felt a coach should rub his own toe. The best way to look at our bruises is to go back to my diary, a personal journal of the season that I never got to finish.

The diary, the first I ever kept, begins the day after Ole Miss upset Arkansas, 27 to 22, in the Sugar Bowl at New Orleans on January 1, 1970.

New Orleans/January 2
Even the strong New Orleans coffee tastes good today. All the Ole Miss people are still hugging each other. With LSU just a few miles up the road with a fine 9-1 team, I don't think many of our people realize how lucky we were to make it here.

Our big wins over Tennessee and LSU did it, but Bob Roesler's column in *The Times-Picayune* this morning noted there had been criticism of an invitation to a 7-3 team. Bob concluded, however, that Ole Miss came through with one of the great games in Sugar Bowl history.

I would like to bring a 10-0 team back here next year.

Oxford/January 9
The publicity about Archie and the team beats anything I've ever seen. Other coaches used to tell me I was lucky to be in a backwash area away from daily newspaper and television coverage. That backwash stuff is hogwash. This morning a Memphis newspaper had three-quarters of a page about Archie's smalltown background. A couple of things in the article caught my eye. The writer said Archie's arm was broken in a football game in his junior year at Drew High School. On the way to the doctor his father asked him if football was worth it. "Yes, dad," Archie said. "This and more." The reporter found this inscription under Archie's picture in the yearbook: "Take care of me—good men are rare." This old coach will buy that.

Washington/January 10
I got to thinking about the days when haircuts cost two-bits at the big banquet tonight. I wish Archie's hair had been clipped a little shorter but otherwise he looked great when he received the Washington Touchdown Club's Walter Camp Memorial Award as the outstanding back in 1969. Tom Harmon, completely gray but still athletic looking, conducted the ceremonies in the Park Sheraton. Last month, just before he went up to Nashville to receive the *Banner's* Most Valuable Player in the SEC award, Archie stopped by my office. I told him to be careful, not to let any newspapermen get him in a corner—and to get a damn haircut. He left laughing and I knew I had lost that one.

Atlanta/January 24
The Atlanta Touchdown Club presented Archie the H. J. Stegeman

Trophy tonight as the finest college back in the south. Earlier in the day, Charlie Trippi said Manning ranks with the most gifted backs in college history. "You can't teach anybody the things he does," Charlie said. "You've got to be born with it. When he gets away with starting left, gets hemmed up, comes back right and either runs or throws for gains or touchdowns that's instinct. Only the great get away with it."

Oxford/February 10
I must be slipping. Gene Hickerson, one of my old players and an All-Pro guard for the Cleveland Browns, stopped by today and we went to lunch at Miller Hall. We got to talking about the blocking assignments on the Cleveland Sweep and I discovered that I had forgotten to bring my notebook. A coach can't do without one, but I used a table napkin. The more I look at the play the more I think Ole Miss will use it this fall.

Gulfport/February 17
Doc Varner, the team physician, and I drove here for Glenn Cannon Day. On the way down I fiddled with some offensive plays in my notebook until Doc said, "Johnny, why don't you let up a little?" He let the subject drop when I said, "Doc, I can't. With all the publicity about Archie and the team I've got to do the best coaching job I've ever done." This is one trip I wanted to make. Glenn Cannon was an All-American safety for us, but it was his dedication that won me. Glenn thinks the 1970 team won't miss him, but it just isn't so.

Oxford/March 21
I sat in the press box to watch the spring game. Luther Webb, a sophomore we're counting on, missed a few holes, but I think he has the ability to be our fullback this fall. He missed the 1969 season because of a leg injury that he received water skiing. Right now, I think Luther will start for us. If he fails, I'll use Bob Knight or Jim Porter. I noticed Jimmy Taylor in the press box. Lord, what a fullback he was at LSU and Green Bay. Maybe there's an omen in seeing Jimmy while trying to rate fullbacks. We've made progress on defense; we'll be better there than we were last year. Some young boys will have to come through, but I see physical ability. We have good competition everywhere and there are seven linebackers to pick from to aid our down people. Safety concerns me, but Danny Hooker has been very aggressive. Dedication is what I'm looking for. I don't want the boys to promise it to me—I want them to say it to each other.

Jackson/March 23

The Jackson Touchdown Club honored Archie tonight as Mississippi's Sportsman of the Year for 1969. Club president Dick Hitt told the audience, "No other athlete in the history of the state has been so consistently outstanding as Manning was throughout the 1969 football season."

Oxford/May 15

Every club and organization you can think of is inviting Archie to talk to them. I met today with Archie's mother, Mrs. Jane Manning, and a Drew lawyer, P. T. Townsend, to discuss all the situations involving Manning. The three of us agreed to act as a clearing house. My concern is that nothing happens to jeopardize Archie's amateur standing. The fast-buck boys started with Archie buttons and have moved on to songs and tee shirts. Archie ignores it, thank the Lord. He knows it won't buy him hamburger. In my senior year I had a small taste of what he's going through. In 1933 two young con men went around Fort Worth and used Lon Evans' name and mine selling space in the TCU yearbook, then skipped town. Lon and I were innocent, but the police pulled us in and scared us to death.

Point Clear, Alabama/May 26

The NCAA asked Archie to join 14 other college players on a tour of Vietnam. He really wanted to go but turned it down to attend summer school. Archie said he wants to graduate with his class next June. That redheaded boy impresses me more each day.

Oxford/July 15

In a letter to the boys today I mentioned some of the publicity they are generating, but I told them I wasn't frightened by it. I think the kids want to live up to public expectations. My boys have the potential to win the Southeastern Conference championship. I sense that they want to go undefeated and share in a once-in-a-lifetime dream. Here's the letter:

> To: Members of the 1970 Ole Miss Varsity Football Team
>
> From: John H. Vaught, Head Football Coach
>
> Many of you will be on campus for the second semester of summer school and I will have an opportunity to see you personally, but I think it is well that we all start thinking in the same direction— toward preparation for our coming '70 season.

We had a fine spring training, and many of you showed considerable improvement. We have been picked to win by the news directors of SEC member institutions. This is quite a compliment and I am not unhappy about this prediction. However, in order to realize this end, it will be necessary that every member of our team be much improved over last year. I want all of you to sincerely dedicate yourself to the coming season with the purpose in mind of giving everything you have, both physically and morally, in order to achieve a once-in-a-lifetime dream.

I want to ask that you start your serious training for our fall work by the first of August. I know it is difficult to work individually to the point of pushing yourself for tough conditioning, but this must be done. You must be ready to go full speed when you report, as we start off real fast in our schedule. Get your weight down to your playing condition, work hard on over-distance, weights and sprints.

I am looking for some real character and leadership from our senior crowd. I am hoping that you will establish an image of your own.

I will write you later this summer, giving you the reporting date. In the meantime, I hope you are having a pleasant summer.

Oxford/August 11

I sent a letter to the boys today telling them the training table would open Wednesday night, August 26. Our first practice is just 17 days away. I still feel good about the team. I think the coaching staff has dedicated itself to doing the best job in my 25 seasons here. Once again, Doc Knight, our trainer, has put us on the spot. His annual inspirational message to the boys already has been mimeographed. It's a series of sentences beginning with these capital letters:

N
A
T
I
O
N
A
L

C
H
A
M
P
I
O
N
S

That Doc! I ought to tape up his typewriter—or make him coach. Here's my note to the boys:

To: Members of the 1970 Ole Miss Varsity Football Team

From: John H. Vaught, Head Football Coach

I hope that you have followed my suggestion in my letter of July 15, relative to your training schedule. I have felt in the past that a small percentage of you have neglected this preparation and, therefore, delayed our team effort. Have you really made an effort toward physically preparing yourself for a tough season? You have a few days left in order to enhance your physical progress, so get with it!

The training table will open for the evening meal on Wednesday, August 26. Thursday will be spent in the taking of physical examinations and pictures. Our first training period will begin at 9:00 a.m. on Friday, August 28,

I am looking forward to seeing you—ready to go!

Memphis/August 22

I came here tonight to see the Kansas City Chiefs play the Cleveland Browns in an exhibition game. A couple of weeks ago I sent two defensive coaches, Roland Dale and Junie Hovious, up to Liberty, Missouri, to study the Kansas City defense. Our linebackers and defensive backs will use some of the techniques developed by the Super Bowl champs.

Oxford/August 27

The boys took their physicals today. Most of them checked in close to their playing weight, but the thing that awes me these days is how tall kids are getting. Thirty boys on the varsity stand 6-2 or taller. Nine are 6-4. Our senior center from Biloxi, Wimpy Winther, checked in at 6-5 and 260 and tight end Jim Poole at 6-5 and 226. Two sophomore tackles, Larry Northam of Vernon, Alabama, and John Thornton of Pascagoula, are 6-4½. Ole Miss has had great success with tall athletes for 25 seasons.

Oxford/September 5

Everyone around the campus is chuckling at the yarn Dr. Porter Fortune, Jr., the university's chancellor, told touring sports writers. Someone asked Dr. Fortune if he had seen Archie's picture with the pre-season All-America squad in *Playboy*. "I was at a meeting in Jackson recently and went to a newsstand to get one," he said, "but a lady I know came along about that time, and I asked the clerk for a copy of the *Christian Science Monitor.* "

Oxford/September 15
Our first game is just four days away. Our middle guard, Paul Dongieux of Jackson, is among the walking wounded with an arch injury, but he's a tough one. He'll play if we need him in the Memphis State game. In practice, Elmer Allen, a 6-3, 230 junior defensive tackle from Delhi, Louisiana, has been tremendous. I can't wait to see him in a game. The heat—there have been numerous days above 90 degrees—has sapped us a little, but I see dedication. The boys will need it in the days ahead. *Sports Illustrated* rated Ole Miss the second best team in the country and said Archie appeared to be the best of many fine quarterbacks. Last week, in a preseason poll, AP put us No. 5, behind Ohio State, Texas, Southern Cal and Arkansas. Those are challenging compliments for the boys. Incidentially, Ole Miss isn't a little school any more. Chancellor Fortune said today that preliminary enrollment had reached 7,013, the highest figure in the history of the university. That's almost 5,000 more students than the school had in 1946 when I first set foot on the campus.

Oxford/September 18
It's 10:30 p.m. now and it's been a long day. Many hours were spent finalizing our game plans. I took a last look at last year's game film with Memphis State. As usual on the day before a game, I reviewed the offensive and defensive check lists and the starting lineups with the staff. We made one lineup change. Ray Heidel, a senior, made a strong comeback in practice after taking a second row to Frank McKellar, a sophomore, at left cornerback. Ray will start. We are going into this game with more offense than usual because we are not sure what Memphis State's defensive alignment will be, and we may have to resort to a definite plan of attack, perhaps an inside running game. But we are ready for a dropback passing game, an option game or a sprint-out attack. Physically, I have been concerned about pulled muscles and bruises. We have had lots of running, but not much team scrimmage. The weather has been real hot, but the attitude has been good. Our punting has been spotty. Both punters—Crowell Armstrong and Larry Northam—have a good foot, but have been inconsistent. They need to boom a few under pressure. Northam wears only a sock on his kicking

foot. Our secondary defense has been a real concern, but I feel we are more knowledgeable about our defense than last year. We have some good young boys that need to win. I'm expecting a hard game from Coach Billy Murphy's Tigers; at the same time I'm looking for a big effort from our lads.

September 19

Ole Miss 47, Memphis State 13

Ole Miss	6	21	7	13	47
MSU	0	0	6	7	13

Memphis/September 19

We were very aggressive against Memphis State tonight, but we made many mistakes. One of the most gratifying things in the game was our defense, but we didn't see a passing quarterback. Some of our young boys showed real promise. Memphis State's linebackers stunted to the outside from the start, leaving their tackles vulnerable to traps by our guards. Archie also utilized the counter play well with our tailback, Randy Reed.

Reed scored twice and Archie hit on 17 of 22 passes for a fine night. Our ability to run up the middle aided our passing game tremendously. It's good to play—and win—that first game. Next week we meet Kentucky and someone told me Coach Ray's team upset Kansas State today. For some reason, Kentucky always plays well against us. Last year at Lexington, the Wildcats upset us, 10-9. They are on my mind and I'm still in Memphis.

Jackson/September 25

I am concerned about the Kentucky game tomorrow. Somehow, this team seems to get sky high for us, and, this year, it is difficult to evaluate Coach Johnny Ray's squad at Kentucky. It lost its first game to North Carolina, but last week it bounced back real big against Kansas State, pulling a major upset despite the passing of Lynn Dickey, K-State's talented quarterback. Kentucky's defense looks devastating. We have worked hard on a game plan to outdo this strong Kentucky defense. We must not make mistakes, such as fumbles and interceptions. We plan to use audibles at the line when a weakness is detected, or when a play called in the huddle appears to stand a small chance for success. Archie has great ability to do this. We have worked hard this week on our kicking game, and it shows improvement. It was lousy in our first game. Our defense has prepared for a strong running game, but we do not yet know how strong our defense is. We do need to put a real good game together. I hope so.

September 26

Ole Miss	7	7	0	6	20
Kentucky	3	6	0	8	17

Jackson/September 26
We did not play with great enthusiasm, although I don't want to take anything from Kentucky, which has a good defensive team. We've got some work to do. We worked the ball down to Kentucky's 5-yard line on two different occasions. But we sputtered there and failed to get anything out of either. Even a field goal at that time could have changed the complexion. Bob Knight ran a punt back for a touchdown and Archie passed for two more to win it for us. Archie was not able to operate at full speed. I haven't gotten the verdict from Doc Knight yet, but Archie appears to have pulled a muscle in his right groin. This kid never quits though. Statistics don't mean much to him; winning does. With 1:33 remaining in the fourth quarter, we got the ball on our 32 yard line. On first down, Archie handed off to Knight, who got five at left tackle. Kentucky called time out. On second and five, Webb plunged for two. This time, when Kentucky called for a time out, Archie came over to the sidelines. This was no place to turn over the football, so I said, "Archie, we've got to have a first down. We've got to have it." He and I both agreed that he should run the ball. Moving behind big Wimpy Winther, our center, Archie made five yards, two more than we needed for the first down. Manning killed the clock with the next four plays and we had our first conference victory. Archie personally took losses on those plays to avoid any possibility of a fumble. This kid deserves each honor that he gets.

Oxford/October 2
We have worked awfully hard this week. One of the major things we did was to study the film of the Kentucky game as close as possible. In doing so, we re-evaluated our personnel. We know we have got to have

better performance and added strength at fullback, where Luther Webb, the sophomore we were counting on heavily, and Scooter Havard, a senior, have been alternating. We have another sophomore fullback, Jim Porter, whose running takes me back to the early 1950's. His running style reminds me of Showboat Boykin. Jim is quick and he may push the other boys before the season ends. There has been no announcement in the newspapers, but Archie is hurting. He has a pulled groin muscle in the right leg. Archie will play, but I'm concerned about him. Billy Reed of *Sports Illustrated* learned about the injury, but his story will appear after the Alabama game tomorrow night in Jackson. This game will be on national television and it appears to be the most important game on our schedule. If we can get by this one, we will be on our way toward winning the SEC championship. Our game plans are set; it's up to us now to get 100 per cent performance out of our players. In all my years at Ole Miss we have never stressed more the importance of defense—and individual execution. It's going to take all that to beat Coach Bear Bryant's bunch.

October 3

Ole Miss	14	12	0	22	48
Alabama	0	9	8	6	23

Jackson/October 3

I am extremely happy with the team's dedication, enthusiasm and desire to win the Alabama game. We came close to putting it all together, with the exception of our punting. Last week, Larry Northam, punting with only a stocking on his right foot, led the conference statistically, but he dribbled one five yards tonight and I told him to put his shoe on. The offense played well, but the defense was superb. The front four—John Gilliland, Elmer Allen, John Aldridge and Dennis Coleman—had a step on the Alabama line most of the night, and the linebackers blew in with ease, throwing the Alabama passers for losses eight times. Crowell Armstrong, Freddy Brister, Jeff Horn and the other linebackers proved themselves. Despite the sore groin, Archie threw three touchdown passes and scored two on the ground. My Black Sheep—but a hell of an athlete—Vernon Studdard ran a kick-off back 101 yards for a TD. He'll remind me of it this coming week. The hard-running of our tailback, Randy Reed, pleased me too. I'd like to savor this victory for a week. Some fan sent the team this telegram:

Have information on best authority that a fuzzy object resembling
an Alabama Bear was seen treading water in the Pearl River attempt-
ing to leave Jackson under cover of darkness. Congratulations
Rebels on such a fine team effort.

There were other telegrams but we must now forget the victory and
start getting ready for a tough battle between the hedges in Athens,
Georgia, next week.

Oxford/October 7
The Associated Press today selected Crowell Armstrong, one of our
linebackers, as national lineman of the week. Crowell, a junior from
Houston, won the honor for tackling Neb Hayden, the Alabama quarterback, behind the line six times for losses totalling 52 yards. Crowell
turned in the best job of linebacking that Ole Miss has had in several
years.

Athens/October 9
One of the hardest things to endure about college football is to fly into
a strange town and wait overnight for a game. I don't like this waiting,
but I've been thinking a lot about the game tomorrow afternoon. I feel
that Georgia is a much better team than its record indicates. Coach
Vince Dooley's boys have lost two games by a total of four points, but
they easily could be going into the game against us undefeated. And
Georgia is double tough here in Athens. Ole Miss must be ready for a
real, real tough game, and expect to meet them head on. I'll say this,
our preparation and concentration this week have been good. Archie is
still bothered with a groin ailment, and we have let him rest for the past
two days. I just hope he is ready to roll tomorrow. Football is a game
of emotions and breaks. Ole Miss must have an enthusiastic effort—and
pray for some breaks.

October 10

Ole Miss	7	7	0	17	31
Georgia	7	7	7	0	21

Oxford/October 10
We flew home immediately after the game and I'm more relaxed
tonight than I have been for the past four weeks. A friend told me I

kept my right hand clenched throughout the third quarter, when we trailed 14 to 21.

I probably did. In the fourth quarter we got a big break. The kickoff after our tying touchdown went untouched by the Georgia deep backs and Ronnie Moses covered it for us at the 13. A motion penalty hurt us, but Cloyce Hinton kicked us into a 24-21 lead with a 36-yard field goal. The lapse by Georgia and Hinton's kick put us in command to stay. Georgia showed me a bloody-nose offense—and a strong defense against the run. We played sluggishly both offensively and defensively the first half, but I was proud of the way our defense played in the second half. There were many things open offensively, but we couldn't execute our option game with quickness and speed because Archie was unable to run full speed. A bright spot was the improvement in our kicking game. Hinton pulled a leg muscle before the Memphis State game, but didn't tell anyone until after he missed two field goal attempts. I had a few stern words with him about that. A coach must know when he has an injured player out there. Jim Poole kicked four-of-four extra points against Georgia. That makes eight straight for him. Our record now is 4-0—and three are SEC victories—but the team still hasn't reached its potential. I'm looking for and expecting more improvement. We should get better on quickness and precision. But it's satisfying to see Archie throw three TDs and run for one more despite an injury that limits his running.

Oxford/October 13

The Associated Press today named Archie SEC back of the week for the second straight week. The award cited touchdown passes of 66, 52 and 9 yards against Georgia, along with a 3-yard run. In four games, Archie has been responsible for 14 touchdowns. His nearest competitors are Bob Parker of Air Force with 13, and Brian Sipe of San Diego State and Dennis Dummit of UCLA, both with 12. All of them have played one more game than Archie.

Oxford/October 16

We will open on our Astroturf tomorrow against Southern Mississippi. We have experimented all week with different cleats in order to find the best traction possible. I am certain of one thing—the turf is much faster than sod. The passing game is different in timing. In general, all reaction is quicker. We will open without Elmer Allen, a good defensive tackle, and Archie is not in top running shape. Our sprint-out attack will be hurt some by that, but our morale has been good and we should expect a good performance from our team. Southern has looked real good offensively. I believe they will be the best passing offense that we have met. They mix the pass with the running game, which presents a problem. We have got to play better defense than we did last week. It doesn't make any difference whom we play or where we play; I'm always concerned. This is football—and anyone can beat you if you are not ready to play. Our punting has looked good all week. It's about time to put a good kicking game together. All of us are concerned about Tad Smith, our athletic director. He is in Lafayette County Hospital with a mild heart attack. The doctors say he was stricken with myocardialischemia, which reduces the blood flow to a small area of heart muscle. We're praying for a quick recovery. Tad hired me 25 years ago and I owe him a lot.

October 17

Ole Miss	14	0	0	0	14
Southern Miss	7	10	13	0	30

Oxford/October 17

I am hurt and embarrassed. Our enthusiasm was nil. I didn't feel well before the game—my 249th at Ole Miss. I told Doc Varner I wasn't up to par, but he gave me a blood pressure test and the reading was normal. I guess I'm coming down with the flu. Losing this game didn't help me a bit. I felt all along that Southern was the best offensive team on our schedule to this date. But I failed; I never got my point across to the boys. When the team got into the dressing room immediately after the game, I put my clipboard down and said, "Congratulations on a great game." You could have heard a pin drop. I never saw a more contrite bunch of kids. These boys have a lot of character—they showed that to me last year after one-point, back-to-back losses to Kentucky and Alabama—but they were not mentally ready today. Of course, this was a tremendous win for Southern Mississippi, surely the biggest in the history of the school. The game story is quickly told by the ground statistics. Ole Miss ran with the ball 41 times for 85 yards. Southern ran with the ball 38 times for 205 yards. Ray Guy averaged 49 yards per punt for Southern to keep us in the hole, offsetting Archie's passing. Archie threw for two first quarter touchdowns, but we just didn't get a consistent ground game to go with his passing. He hit on 30 of 56 attempts for 341 yards, but Archie simply is not Archie when he is unable to run at full speed. Next week we move back into the SEC against Vanderbilt, and some changes must be made. We'll have to wait and see after we have studied the film. Senior leadership, one of the things I've always counted on, failed to measure up to its capabilities. I wish we had juniors and sophomores pushing them harder. Southern's coach, P. W. Underwood, characterized the game rather aptly when he told newsmen, "We took it to their butt and we whipped their butt." I won't argue about it; it was Southern's day. I think this Ole Miss team will want to be winners from here on out. We are hurt and embarrassed tonight though.

That was the last entry in my diary. An overwhelming turn in my life was approaching.

The victory over Ole Miss led Coach Underwood to the honorary mayorship of Hattiesburg. I don't want to diminish his glory, but my team should have whipped his by three touchdowns. The loss has to be classed as one of the upsets of the century in college football. An old friend of mine, Fred Russell of the *Nashville Banner*, saw it this way:

> All factors considered—the rankings, the battle site, the score— Mississippi Southern's 30-14 stunner at Ole Miss could be the South's most astonishing football upset of all-time, or at least covering the past 50 years.
>
> For a worthy parallel, one must go back to little Centre College's 6-0 victory over Harvard in 1921. Closer home, there's Sewanee's 16-0 bopping of Vanderbilt on Thanksgiving Day, 1924, five days after the Commodores had downed then-mighty Minnesota, 16-0.

I hate to be a part of that kind of history. I didn't sleep a wink the night after the worse debacle in my coaching career. Looking back on that disastrous October day, I may have been too sick to coach. When Doc Varner, who lives in Memphis, came into my office, he said, "How you feeling?"

"My body is sore all over, Doc," I replied. "I'm completely exhausted."

Neither of us had an inkling of what lay ahead. Going into

the dressing room after the game I slammed my right fist against the metal door and knocked it open. A terrible mood possessed me. Ole Miss—the fourth-ranked college team in the nation—had lost to an inferior team. That meant one thing to me. My boys weren't properly motivated. Football is a game of emotion and motivation, and after four tension-filled games, Ole Miss got lulled to sleep. I sensed this as we prepared for Southern. I tried to undo it, but I failed.

After the game I told the staff we had suffered the greatest defeat in Ole Miss football—and full blame should be placed on me for not motivating the team through them.

Southern caught us flatfooted. Archie took the field in terrible physical shape. To heal, a pulled groin needs rest, but there had been none of that for Archie since the Kentucky game. If he had been able to run anywhere close to par he would have scored three touchdowns on the ground. But he failed to get the ball across, and the team began to break down from lack of aggressiveness. Our starting left tackle, Elmer Allen, missed the game because of a leg injury, but I don't want to make excuses. Southern took to Hemingway Stadium sky high. As a result, the 5-0 halfway mark that every man, woman and child in Mississippi expected of Ole Miss turned into a bitter 4-1 situation.

One of the hardest jobs in coaching is getting your boys up for a game that sportswriters call a warmup. And unfortunately, you can't always turn things around at halftime by saying, "Come on, let's go get 'em, girls."

I was determined to bring the team back. Despite the lack of sleep, I returned to my office at 9 a.m. Sunday and began running film. The movies told me we had to switch our backfield around. Our fullbacks simply couldn't get the job done. I decided to take our two tailbacks and make one a fullback. Randy Reed, the No. 1 tailback, moved to fullback. His backup, Bob Knight, became the starting tailback. We didn't want our next opponent, Vanderbilt, to know this, and no announcement was made. The films also clearly revealed poor defensive play and a lack of agressiveness by the entire squad.

The keyed up Southern team rippled with aggressiveness. And, surprisingly, it played an errorless game despite the high emotional pitch. The Southern punter kicked us to death, too.

When the last film reel stopped it was 2 a.m. I didn't say anything to the other coaches but my body ached all over. My staff and I worked until midnight Monday on our Vanderbilt game plan, which included a stepped up passing attack as well as the switch involving the running backs. I planned more night work Tuesday and I ate supper in the athletic dorm cafeteria. As I left the dining room I caught myself staggering. Billy Mustin, an assistant coach, saw me bump a chair and said, "Coach, you're tripping over everything."

I brushed off the comment and went back to the office, where we ran film until 9 p.m. Then a touch of nausea hit me. "Boys," I said to my assistants, "I'm sick. I've got to go home."

I drove the five miles to my farm and crawled into bed. It was about 10 p.m. when I turned to my wife and said: "Johnsie, there's something wrong with me."

She sat up. "How do you feel?"

"My arms are aching and I have a nauseous feeling in my chest."

Johnsie got out of bed, saying, "I'm calling Jerry." Dr. Jerry Hopkins, one of the team physicians, lived in Oxford.

"You don't need to call him," I said. "I just need an antacid."

Johnsie wouldn't listen and Dr. Hopkins got to the farm about 11 p.m. He suggested that I go to the hospital, but I didn't want to go. I knew he would keep me away from the Vanderbilt game in Nashville. I hadn't missed a game since 1946. But I could see that Jerry was concerned. He had put a nitroglycerin tablet under my tongue and I had felt immediate relief. Then he gave me a couple of shots and talked me into his car. He drove me to the Oxford-Lafayette County Hospital. Jerry diagnosed my trouble as a heart circulation problem but I shut the idea out of my mind for seven days.

While in the hospital, I listened to the Vandy game by radio. The boys won, 26 to 16 in a downpour, but I felt awful lying there flat of my back. I was determined to be back on the practice field to get ready for Houston which was two weeks away. I left the hospital after a week and I got Jerry to agree to let me come to my office for an hour and to go on the practice field for an hour in a golf cart.

I didn't tell anyone, but I had a mild recurrence in chest pains the second night after I returned to work. The next night, Sunday, November 1, the pains hit even harder. Finally, I decided to tell Johnsie—to confess really. We sat at a table and looked each other in the eye. "Johnsie," I said, "I want you to call Jerry and get him out here. I've got to lay things on the table."

Dr. Hopkins is a tremendous physician. I have every confidence in him. We talked and both agreed that I needed more tests. He knew I had to be convinced about what was wrong. As it turned out, Jerry was right from the start. We put in a call to Doc Varner in Memphis to get his recommendation on a cardiologist, and a few hours later I was in the intensive care unit at Methodist Hospital in Memphis, where Dr. J. B. Witherington kept me until moving me to a private room the following Thursday. He came up with the same diagnosis as Jerry. I had a major circulatory problem. An artery around or outside the heart was not getting enough blood.

I didn't know it at the time, but I had coached my last football game at Ole Miss. In the hospital I listened to the Houston game on radio. I was highly sedated and fought to keep mentally alert, but from time to time I passed John Glenn or some other astronaut in orbit.

When Archie got hurt, it upset the hell out of me. He's the finest athlete I've seen in my life, bar none—college or pro. The team turned in a tremendous game against Houston, winning 24 to 13, but Archie received a broken left arm when struck by two Cougars as he passed. Within hours he was in Memphis Baptist Hospital for surgery. We were four blocks apart and I talked to him by telephone. The following Monday Archie underwent two hours of surgery by Dr. Marcus Stewart, a well known orthopedic surgeon. He inserted a special Swiss-made compression plate above the broken radius in Archie's arm. The plate, held by four screws, compressed both ends of the broken bone together. This creates a smaller gap or crack in the bone and speeds the mending process. Archie, the first round draft pick of the New Orleans Saints will wear this through his first pro season. It will be taken out when the season ends.

Bruiser Kinard, my offensive line coach and one of the greatest names in football, took over as interim coach after I became ill. He faced a difficult regrouping task on the heels of the Southern disaster. I helped him to set up the Vanderbilt game plans, but after the Houston game I lost all contact with preparations until the Gator Bowl game.

My recovery came slowly. I was lying in a hospital bed thinking about the team and the realization that I couldn't do a thing to help made me despondent. I had known the relationship of emotions and results in football games for a long time, but it took weeks of hospitalization and medical treatment to see the link between emotional stress and illness. From October 20, 1970, the date of my first hospitalization, to January 21, 1971, the day I officially became football coach emeritus at Ole Miss, I had to learn to live with my condition. The only bright spots late in 1970 came when the team whipped Chattanooga, 44 to 7, and the Gator Bowl later invited Ole Miss to play Auburn in Jacksonville on January 2, 1971. It was Ole Miss' 14th consecutive bowl invitation, something no other team in the nation has been able to accomplish. I got out of Methodist Hospital on November 22 but I couldn't do much but sit around the house and mope. My emotions were shot to pieces when Ole Miss— for only the second time in 24 seasons—lost to Mississippi State, 19 to 14, on Thanksgiving Day, and to LSU on December 5 by a horrendous score, 61 to 17. For me, Archie Manning won his badge of courage in the LSU game. Few men have ever taken to a football field under such handicaps. His dedication will take him far.

In my own situation, a paradox had developed. I had planned to quit after the 1970 season, but as I struggled to recover from my illness I felt a burning desire to continue coaching. I was 61 but I thought of certain young men who would be playing. That was in the back of my mind when I signed a new four-year contract as head football coach and assistant athletic director on November 26. Tad Smith, our athletic director who had come back from a heart problem but had reached retirement age, also signed for one more year at the request of Chancellor Porter Fortune.

I even got into recruiting. Greenwood had a tall, talented high school quarterback in Bill Malouf, and on December 11 I went down to that Delta city, spent the night in a Holiday Inn under someone else's name and signed Bill the next day.

Two days later I called a squad meeting to talk about the Gator Bowl. I asked the other coaches to stay away; I wanted to face them alone. I didn't make a big speech, but I told the boys about the traditions of the University of Mississippi and pride. I told them our bowl record and our national television image were part of their heritage. I told them of the many good things that come from a fine performance.

Ole Miss lost, 35-28, in the highest-scoring game in Gator Bowl history, but Archie and his teammates won a measure of national respect by fighting back from a 21-0 deficit. My doctors wouldn't let me go to the game, but I watched on television.

With the first days of 1971 ticking by I resembled a lost boy. I was taking a lot of medicine and my trips to the doctor were discouraging. As January wore on, I could see that Chancellor Fortune and Tad were waiting for a signal from me. The sports publicity department was receiving calls from sportswriters asking when spring practice would start.

I stalled. I simply didn't know what I was going to do. I resented the fact that illness was forcing me out. I had never even had a bad headache before this thing, and I wanted to defeat it. Published reports said that I was forced out, but anyone familiar with the situation at Ole Miss knows the facts are otherwise. The truth is that my coaching career ended on Wednesday, January 13, 1971, in the office of Dr. Hopkins in Oxford. That is the day I knew it was over. Jerry put it to me bluntly. He said my physical condition could not stand the stress and strain that are inherent along the sidelines. He said he thought it would be fatal to continue.

It was the first time he had used the word "fatal." When he told me this I wasn't surprised. I was hurt, of course. I wanted to return. I left the doctor's office and went back to the athletic department to talk to my old friend, Tad, who had hired me in 1947. I think he suspected the worst. Tad had planned to stay on as Athletic Director for another year despite his own health problem, but he looked at me and said: "John, if you can't coach I will retire and you can be the athletic director."

I told Tad I wasn't sure I could do that work. Finally, the athletic committee reviewed the situation, giving special attention to my illness. It asked Tad to talk to me and see if I would be happy if it retired me on emeritus status under the present coaching contract. I thought it over and finally told Tad nothing could make me happier. My single condition was that my staff—which had helped me to build a winner at Ole Miss—be taken care of.

There were tears in Tad's eyes and mine. Tad said he would step out too, and then recommended that Bruiser become athletic director. I thought the university would benefit by a long range situation. Even if my health allowed it, I could serve only four more years. My real interest is in the University of Mississippi; I want it to grow and prosper.

Once Bruiser took over as athletic director, I stepped out of the picture. The selection of the new coach and formulation of the staff were in his hands. No announcement of all this had been made, and a few days later Bruiser came to my office and brought up the name of his younger brother, Billy Kinard, who had played on our 1956 Cotton Bowl winner. "I'm bringing in Billy for an interview," Bruiser said. I told him, "That's fine with me." Shortly thereafter Bruiser placed two names before the athletic committee—Billy Kinard, then a defensive secondary coach at the University of Arkansas, and Bob Tyler, the fine young flanker coach on our staff who shared an office with Bruiser. When the committee was told that Billy was Bruiser's first choice, it named him head coach. All of these moves had to be approved by the state Board of Trustees before any announcement could be made, but I called my staff together to tell them of the impending news.

I told them I would like to continue coaching but that it was a physical impossibility. Someone spoke up immediately and asked if I was moving up to Athletic Director. "That's out too," I said.

That shocked them, I saw, because I had preached staff togetherness for so long. Everyone in the room felt the staff that had helped Ole Miss climb a steep hill should be disturbed as little as possible. I assured them that Bruiser wanted it that way and that all of them would be taken care of by the university. I also told them I felt that Billy Kinard, who came out of our football family and had kept in touch with it through the years, would want them to stay.

Frankly, I feel good about the future of the University of Mississippi in football. My own mind is at peace. As football coach emeritus and assistant athletic director, I'm looking forward to a public relations role for the next four years. When all the changes were announced officially on January 21 in Jackson, the state capital, I felt much better.

I went to sleep that night without any medical inducement for the first time in three months. That convinced me that stress and tension had been part of my recovery problem. But the past 25 years at Ole Miss have been worth all the emotional wear and tear.

22

A Summing Up

Since 1893 the head football coaches at Ole Miss have come from such schools as Rutgers, Notre Dame and Stanford. In 1971 the Rebels will be led by an Ole Miss graduate—Billy Kinard—for the first time. Billy played on my 1956 Cotton Bowl team and he knows the value of our big Rebel family.

Looking back on my career, I consider myself a fundamentalist, not a mossback. I believe in perfection of execution—in the blocking and tackling angles of the game. But there's more to it. The worst thing a football coach can do is to stand pat, to think the plays and formations that worked yesterday will win tomorrow. Intelligent changes must be made.

I have seen college football change with American society during the past 25 seasons. The crying towel has disappeared. Remember the days of "Weeping Wally" Butts at Georgia? I used to be the same way. In my early years at Ole Miss I used to dread for my teams to receive top billing in the conference. But I changed. Practically all college coaches have made an about face in their recruiting and training philosophy. Only a few years back, most coaches forced and drove. Today, the successful coach leads and sells.

Football everywhere is a much more spectacular and appealing game today than it was in 1946, and the credit must go to the boys coming into our colleges and universities. Almost without exception, the best athletes are serious students and ambitious. Each boy knows he has to prepare himself to accomplish something in our complex society. Twenty-five years ago, a boy—and his coach—didn't think too much about the future. The future took care of itself. That attitude has disappeared, and the nation is better for it. Because of this change, coaching is easier and a lot more fun.

At Ole Miss I see no indication that football has switched to the day of the easy rider. They kids we get today aren't just big and tall—they have intelligence and awareness. This is the era of the anti-hero, I read, but there must be millions who think differently. Archie Manning, a modest boy with rather long hair, gets fan mail from around the world. Since 1968, Archie has received more letters and invitations to speak than all other Ole Miss stars put together. And, when you think back, that includes Charley Conerly and Jake Gibbs, boys who symbolized the best in college football at the beginning and middle of my years at Oxford. Part of this, of course, rests with Archie's ability. But newspaper, radio and television coverage of Ole Miss teams seems to increase each year. To the nation's football fans, Oxford is as identifiable as South Bend, Austin, Columbus, Pasadena, Baton Rouge and East Lansing.

I don't think that means overemphasis. I think it is good for the University of Mississippi. My goal is for Ole Miss football to be a credit to a fine institution. If it ever becomes anything else, I don't want any part of it.

I like to think that Ole Miss plays good football, that it is making a contribution to a game that has fascinated me since 1925. The Ole Miss coaching staff operates on the theory that you can be genial while teaching boys all the details. But winners never loaf. If Ole Miss must have a label or trademark I want it to be thoroughness in preparation.

In 1960—the year the writers picked Ole Miss as the best team in the nation—I told a newsman that I would never leave Oxford. But, to be truthful, I really made that decision back in 1950 when it would have been so easy to walk away from a job that was just beginning and causing many sleepless nights.

But I stayed. After 20 years of reflection, that has to be the wisest decision I ever made. The credit must go to my Mississippians—my football players. I love them all.

OLE MISS FOOTBALL LETTERMEN

(1946-1970)

A

Adams, Billy Ray, 1959-60-61
Adams, Robert O., 1952-53-54
Aldridge, John, 1968-69-70
Aldridge, Walter P., 1962-63-64
Ainsworth, Greg, 1970
Alford, John Warner, 1958-59-60
Allen, Elmer, 1969-70
Alliston, George B., 1966
Alliston, Vaughn S., Jr., 1953-54-55
Anderson, James N., 1958-59-60
Armstrong, Crowell, 1969-70

B

Bagwell, Mike, 1970
Bailey, Robert W., 1966-67-68
Baker, Jerry E., 1954-55-56
Ball, Warren N., 1958-59-60
Barber, John T., 1954
Barfield, Kenneth A., 1950-51
Barkley, William Donald, 1955-57
Barnett, Eddie Lee, 1967
Basham, William Earl, 1959-60-61
Baskin, John, 1969
Beatty, Edwin M., 1951-52-53
Beddingfield, Wm. Ray, 1963-64-65
Benton, Robert Hollis, 1958-59-60
Bidgood, Charles S., 1947-48
Bishop, Clark D., 1949
Black, Willis W., 1954
Blackwell, Bernard, 1944-45-46-47
Blair, Earl E., 1952-53-54-55
Blair, George L., 1958-59-60
Blalack, John, 1954-55-56
Blount, Clayton, 1946
Blount, Joseph L., 1967-68-69
Blount, Kenneth, 1970
Boggan, Rex Reed, 1949-50, 1954
Bolin, Treva, 1960-61
Boone, James, 1970
Booth, Carl C., 1968

Bourne, Robert, 1961
Bowen, John H., Jr., 1946-47-48
Bowen, John H., III, 1967-68-69
Bowman, Gayle, 1955
Boyd, Robert, 1962
Boykin, A. L., 1949-50-51
Bradley, Bruce, 1949-50
Brashier, Rodgers, 1952-53-54
Brenner, George, 1950-51-52
Brewer, John Lee, 1957, 1959-60
Brewer, William E., 1957-58-59
Bridgers, David I., 1946-47
Bridgers, David I., Jr., 1968-69-70
Bridges, James T., 1951-52
Brister, Fred E. III, 1968-69-70
Brister, Thomas S., 1961
Broussard, Ken G., 1965
Brown, Allen, 1962-63-64
Brown, Carter, 1952
Brown, Ernie, 1970
Brown, Fred, 1946
Brown, Jerry G., 1959-60-61
Brown, Raymond L., 1955-56-57
Brown, William Van, 1967-68
Buchanan, Oscar W., 1946-47-48
Burke, Charles G., Jr., 1955, 1957
Burke, Robert, 1969-70
Burleson, Charles, 1952
Bush, Alan, 1965-66-67
Byrd, Ronard K., 1949-50-51

C

Caldwell, James T., 1950-51-52
Callahan, Lindy, 1949-50-51
Campbell, Henry A., 1948
Cannon, Glenn, 1967-68-69
Carpenter, Preston, 1969-70
Carpenter, Terry Carol, 1967
Carter, Raymond, 1965
Case, Harry, 1956
Caston, Lester Brent, 1964-65-66
Cavin, Jack O., 1958

Champion, James E., 1957-58-59
Champion, William L., 1960, 1962
Chandler, Johnny, 1970
Childres, Robert D., 1952-53
Chisholm, Charles, 1964
Chumbler, Brent, 1969-70
Chunn, Clifton B., Jr., 1968
Churchwell, Hanson, 1957-58
Clark, James H., 1947-48-49
Clay, William F., 1963-64-65
Coker, William H., 1968-69-70
Coleman, Dennis, 1968-69-70
Collier, John, 1969
Collier, Terry Lee, 1967
Conerly, Charles, 1942, 1946-47
Cooper, Harold, 1956-57-58
Cothren, Paige, 1954-55-56
Coward, Charles, 1967
Cox, Owen, 1950
Crain, Milton, 1956-57-58
Crawford, Edward S., 1954-55-56
Crawford, James A., 1946-47-48-49
Crawford, Othar, 1947, 1949-50-51
Crespino, Robert, 1958-59-60
Crosby, Wm. F., 1961-62
Crull, Luther P., 1968
Cunningham, Julian D., 1964-65-66
Curland, Marvin, 1946

D

Dabbs, Willis N., 1960-61-62
Dale, Roland H., 1945, 1947-48-49
Daniels, Jerry, 1958-59-60
Davis, Curtis Reed, 1961-62-63
Davis, Harry, 1949-50
Davis, Paul, 1942, 1946
Day, Herman "Eagle", 1953-54-55
Dean, William J., 1962-63-64
Deaton, Daniel Bernard, 1969
Dennis, Walter M. "Mike", 1963-64-65
Dickerson, Cecil R., 1946
Dickerson, David L., 1952-53-54
Dickson, Donald, 1960-61-62
Dill, Kenneth, 1960-61-62-63
Dill, Reginald, 1970
Dillard, Wilson, 1950-51-52

Dillingham, Bruce, Jr., 1965-66-67
Dongieux, Paul A., Jr., 1969-70
Dottley, John, 1947-48-49-50
Doty, Arthur, 1960-61
Drewry, Robert G., 1953-54-55
Dubuisson, Gene H., 1953-54-55
Duck, Charles, 1955-56
Dunaway, James K., 1960-61-62
Dunn, Perry Lee, 1961-62-63

E

Elmore, James Douglas, 1959-60-61
Erickson, W. C., 1946-47

F

Fagan, Julian W., III, 1967-68-69
Fant, Frank, 1947-48-49
Farber, Louis, 1967-68-69
Farmer, Fred R., 1968-69-70
Farmer, James J., 1966-67
Farragut, Kenneth D., 1947-48-49-50
Farrar, Donald H., 1968, 1970
Felts, Morris Leon, 1968-69
Ferrill, Charles B., 1960
Fisher, Bobby F., 1954-55
Fleming, Gorden W., Jr., 1964-65-66
Fletcher, Robert J., 1947-48-49-50
Flowers, Charles, 1957-58-59
Ford, Cecil A., 1961-62-63
Fowler, Ronald M., 1964-65-66
Frame, J. S., 1965
Franklin, Bobby Ray, 1957-58-59
Franks, Dwayne, 1970
Franks, Floyd, 1968-69-70
Fuerst, Robert J., 1947-48-49

G

Galey, Charles D., 1945-46-47
Garner, Ernest L. "Lee", Jr., 1964-65-66
Garrigues, Robert M., 1966-67-68
Gary, Oscar Knox, Jr., 1951-52
Gates, Hunter, 1946
Garner, John, 1968
Gerrard, Albert L., Jr., 1945, 1949

Gibbs, Jerry D. "Jake", 1958-59-60
Gilbert, Kline, 1950-51-52
Gilliland, John L., 1968-69-70
Glover, Will H., 1947
Goehe, Richard, 1953-54-55
Graham, Michael F., 1965
Grantham, J. Larry, 1957-58-59
Graves, Joe E., 1965-66
Graves, Sam E. III, 1966-67
Green, Allen L., 1958-59-60
Greenlee, Max H., 1964
Gregory, George H., Jr., 1958
Gregory, John A., 1970
Griffing, Glynn, 1960-61-62
Guy, Louis B., 1960-61-62

H

Haddock, James W., 1965, 1967
Haik, Michel, 1965-66-67
Halbert, Frank R., 1960-61
Hall, James S., 1957-58-59
Hall, William Whaley, 1961-62-63
Hamley, Douglas, 1946-47-48-49
Harbin, Leon C., Jr., 1954-55-56
Harper, Everette L., 1945-46-47
Harris, George, 1952-53-54
Harris, Wayne, 1964
Harrison, Glenn, 1968
Hart, Granville, 1950
Harthcock, Billy H., 1966-67
Hartzog, Hugh Miller, Jr., 1967-68-69
Harvey, James, 1963-64-65
Heidel, James, 1963-64-65
Heidel, Ray, 1968-69-70
Heidel, Roy, 1963-64-65
Hemphill, Robert E., 1948-49
Hendrix, Robert E., Jr., 1965-66-67
Herard, Claude, 1967-68-69
Hickerson, Robert Gene, 1955-56-57
Hickerson, Willie Wayne, 1957
Hindman, Stanley, 1963-64-65
Hindman, Stephen, 1966-67-68
Hinton, Charles, 1964-65-66
Hinton, Cloyce, 1969-70
Hitt, Billy, 1951-52
Holder, Owen, 1968

Holloway, A. J., 1960-61-62
Holston, John C., 1958
Hooker, Danny, 1968-69-70
Horn, Jeffrey, 1968-69-70
Hovater, Nobel Owen, 1964
Howell, Earl O., 1947-48
Howell, Ray Jr., 1950-51-52
Huff, Earl, 1955
Humphrey, William R., 1950
Hurst, William Otis, 1955-56-57

I

Ingram, James E., 1950-51-52
Irwin, Billy Carl, 1962-63-64

J

Jabour, Robert, 1948-49-50
James, Edward T., Jr., 1965-66-67
James, Elwyn, 1969
James, Raymond L., 1952-53-54
Jenkins, Eulas S., 1946-47-48-49
Jenkins, Robert L., 1954
Jenkins, Warren D., 1957-58
Jennings, David S., 1962, 1964
Jernigan, Arthur F., Jr., 1968-69-70
Jernigan, Frank, 1951-52-53
Johnson, Joe C., 1944, 1947
Johnson, Larry Leo, 1961-62-63
Jones, Billy Ray, 1959-60-61
Jones, George F., 1968-69-70
Jones, Walter William III, 1967-68-69
Jordan, Bill R., 1970

K

Kelly, James A., 1951-52
Kempinska, Charles C., 1957-58-59
Keyes, Jimmy E., 1965-66-67
Khayat, Robert, 1957-58-59
Kimbrell, Fred T., Jr., 1962
Kinard, Billy R., 1952-53-54-55
Kinard, Frank M., Jr., 1962-63-64
King, Michael, 1969-70
King, Perry Lee, 1968-69
King, Stark, 1966

Kirk, Ken H., 1957-58-59
Knight, Bobby, 1969-70

L

Laird, Charles D., 1960
Lamar, Wayne Terry, 1959-60
Lambert, Franklin T., 1962-63-64
Langston, Thomas E., 1950
Lanter, Lewis, 1961-62
Lear, James H., 1950-51-52
LeBlanc, Allen, 1969-70
Lentjes, Fred W., 1959-60-61
Lewis, William I., 1966
Linton, Henry, Jr., 1951-52-53
Little, Jamie Ray, 1964
Lofton, Harol, 1951-52-53
Lott, Billy Rex, 1955-56-57
Lotterhos, George T., 1968-69-70
Lovelace, Kent E., 1957-58
Lucas, Thomas E., 1962, 1964-65
Luke, Tommy, 1964-65-66

Mc

McClure, Wayne L., 1965-66-67
McClure, Worthy, 1968-69-70
McCool, Robert A., 1952-53-54
McCraney, James, 1966
McKaskel, Jerry D., 1955
McKay, Henry Earl, 1954-55-56
McKay, Rush, 1960-61
McKellar, Frank, 1970
McKibbens, Thomas R., Jr., 1968
McKinney, Bob L., 1952-53-54
McQueen, Marvin E., Jr., 1964-65-66

M

Maddox, John C., 1963-64-65
Magee, Robert M., 1965-66-67
Magee, Thomas, 1969-70
Majure, Toby, 1946
Mangum, Ernest G., 1951-52-53
Mann, B. F., 1946-47
Manning, E. Archie, 1968-69-70
Mask, James E., 1950-51-52

Massey, Charles P., 1949, 1951
Matthews, James R., 1952
Matthews, E. William Jr., 1965-66-67
Mattina, Rodney A., 1962-63-64
Maxwell, Harold L., 1949-50-51
May, Jerry L., 1951-52
Metz, John S., 1964
Millette, T. J., 1950
Mills, Wilmer R., 1964
Milstead, Don M., 1968
Mims, Crawford, 1951-52-53
Mims, Marvin T., 1964
Mitchell, Adam H., Jr., 1968-69-70
Mitchell, John I., Jr., 1959, 1961
Moley, Stanley, 1970
Monsour, Tom, 1970
Montgomery, Charles L., 1950-51-52
Morgan, Gerald, 1957
Morganti, Charles, 1951-52
Morris, Charles, 1960-61-62
Morrow, George C., 1967-68-69
Mosby, Herman, 1969-70
Moses, Ronald, 1970
Moses, Samuel S., Jr., 1963-64
Muirhead, Allen, 1951-52-53-54
Mustin, Robert W., 1946-47-48-49
Myers, Charles W., 1964-65
Myers, Riley, 1968-69

N

Neely, Charles Wyck, 1968-69-70
Nelson, James M., 1963-64-65
Newell, R. Bruce, 1965-66-67
Norman, Charles R., 1965-66
Northam, Larry, 1970

O

Odom, Jack L., 1947-48
Oswalt, Robert J., 1946-47-48
Ott, Dennis H., 1952-53
Ott, Reggie, 1951-52
Owen, Joe Sam, 1969
Owen, Robert L., 1968
Owen, Sam Walton, 1961-62
Owens, Robert L., 1957-58-59

P

Parker, Edd Tate, 1951-52-53
Parkes, James C., Jr., 1966-67-68
Partridge, C. K., 1957-58-59
Paslay, Lea C., 1951-52-53, 1956
Patton, Houston, 1953-54-55
Patton, James R., Jr., 1952-53-54
Pearson, Thomas H., 1947-48-49
Pettey, Thomas J., 1962-63-64
Phillips, Hermon B., 1947
Poole, Calvin Phillip, 1946-47-48
Poole, George Barney, 1942, 1947-48
Poole, Jack L., 1948-49
Poole, James E., Jr., 1969-70
Poole, Oliver L., 1946
Poole, Ray S., 1941-42, 1946
Pope, Carl Allen, 1965
Porter, James, 1970
Powell, Kenneth W., 1960
Powell, Travis, 1962
Powers, Jimmy T., 1954
Price, James Richard, 1958-59-60
Pruett, Billy R., 1955-56-57

R

Randall, George M., 1961-62-63
Rayborn, Jerry Joe, 1963
Reed, John B., 1951-52
Reed, Randy, 1969-70
Reed, S. Leroy, Jr., 1955-56-57
Regan, George Bernie, 1959
Richardson, Jerry Dean, 1965-66-67
Richardson, John A., 1964-65
Robbins, Michael D., 1966-67
Roberson, Shed H., Jr., 1958-59
Roberts, David, 1969
Roberts, Fred F., Jr., 1961-62-63
Roberts, James B., 1960-61-62
Roberts, Kelly, 1965
Robertson, Joseph E., 1958-59-60
Robertson, Reginald M., 1960
Robinson, Bobby D., 1962-63-64
Robinson, John W., 1958-59-60
Rodgers, Paul C., 1950
Ross, Richard D., 1960-61-62

S

Salley, David W., 1950
Salley, James W., 1950
Salmon, Farley, 1945-46-47-48
Sanders, Aubrey, 1957-58
Sartin, Daniel, 1965-66-67
Saul, James K., 1965-66
Sharp, L. V., 1951
Shelby, John, 1942, 1948
Shepherd, Archie, 1952-53-54
Shows, H. N., 1966-67-68
Shows, James Larry, 1964-65-66
Shumaker, Michael, 1968
Simmons, Doug, 1969
Simpson, Jack M., 1955-56-57
Sinquefield, Melvin, 1950-51
Slay, James, 1950-51-52
Smith, E. J., 1956-57-58
Smith, H. A., 1942, 1946
Smith, Kenneth, 1963-64-65
Smith, Ralph A., 1959-60-61
Smith, Ralph G., 1963
Smith, Thomas Larry, 1961-62-63
Spears, James W., 1958
Spiers, Tommy, 1952
Stallings, Danny, 1970
Stewart, H. F., 1966-67
Stolt, John J., 1955
Stone, Henry Jerry, 1954-55-56
Straughn, Robert, 1951
Street, Donald E., 1965-66-67
Stribling, James A., 1946-47-48-49
Stribling, Majure B., 1945, 1948-49-50
Stubblefield, Jerry, 1965
Studdard, Vernon A., 1968-69-70
Sullivan, Charles J., 1966-67
Sullivan, L. Wesley, 1960-61
Sumrall, William W., 1962-63-64
Swetland, Michael R., 1965-66-67

T

Taylor, Charles, 1960-61
Taylor, Harry, 1948
Taylor, Leslie Edward, Jr., 1965-66-67
Taylor, Tommy, 1956-57-58

Tempfer, J. G., 1961
Templeon, Billy, 1956-57-58
Terracin, Steve W., 1964-65-66
Terrell, Marvin J., 1957-58-59
Terrell, James M., 1962
Terry, Decker, 1957-58
Thaxton, James C., 1964
Thomas, Dalton, 1954
Thomas, James Larry, 1968-69
Thornton, James Ray, 1951
Tiblier, Jerome J., 1944, 1947-48
Tillery, Douglas, 1962
Tillman, Ronald, 1965
Torgerson, Larry D., 1968-69-70
Trapp, Frank W., 1966-67-68
Trauth, Marvin H., 1950-51-52
Truett, George W., 1952
Tuggle, Jimmy, 1952
Turner, John H., Jr., 1964

U

Upchurch, Robert K., 1961-62-63
Urbanek, James E., 1965-66-67
Uzzle, Robert H., 1966-67-68

V

Van Devender, Wm. J., 1968-69-70
Vaughan, Robert C., 1965-66-67

W

Wade, Bobby, 1965-66-67
Walker, H. Carroll, Jr., 1965-66

Wallis, James H., 1967-68-69
Walsh, Henry, 1970
Walters, James A., 1953-54
Warfield, Gerald, 1964-65-66
Watson, Billy E., 1949-50-51
Weatherly, James D., 1962-63-64
Webb, Luther, 1970
Webb, Reed S., 1966-67
Weiss, Richard, 1952-53-54-55
Wells, David K., 1963-64-65
West, Carl E., 1950-51
Westerman, Richard, 1950-51-52
White, James T., 1960
Whitener, Larry J., 1966-67
Whiteside, Paul L., 1951
Wilford, Dan, 1961
Wilford, Ned, 1961
Wilkins, Joseph T. III, 1962-63-64
Williams, Don N., 1955-56-57
Williams, John C., Jr., 1954-55
Williams, Murray L., Jr., 1968
Wilson, Robert, 1946-47-48-49
Windham, Donald W., 1962-63-64
Winstead, Bobby, 1968
Winston, Lowell, 1957
Winther, Richard, 1969-70
Wohlgemuth, John, 1970
Woodruff, James Lee, 1957-58-59
Worsham, Jerry D., 1963

Y

Yelverton, Billy G., 1952, 1954-55-56
Young, Carl R., 1949-50
Young, John William, Jr., 1970

All Americans

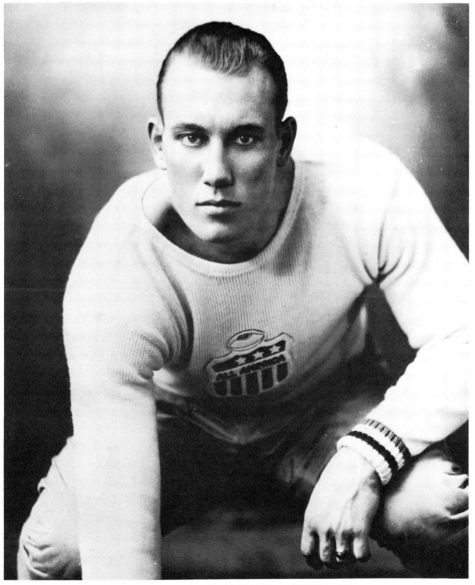

FRANK M. (BRUISER) KINARD
TACKLE   1936-37

PARKER HALL
HALF-BACK   1938

CHARLES CONERLY
HALF-BACK   1947

BARNEY POOLE
END   1947-48

KLINE GILBERT
TACKLE 1952

CRAWFORD MIMS
GUARD   1953

REX REED BOGGAN
TACKLE   1954

JACKIE SIMPSON
GUARD   1957

CHARLIE FLOWERS
FULL-BACK   1959

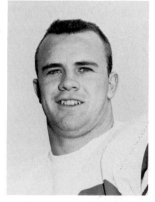

MARVIN TERRELL
GUARD   1959

JAKE GIBBS
QUARTERBACK 1960

BILLY RAY ADAMS
FULL-BACK   1961

GLYNN GRIFFING
QUARTERBACK   1962

JIM DUNAWAY
TACKLE   1962

WHALEY HALL
TACKLE   1963

KENNY DILL
CENTER   1963

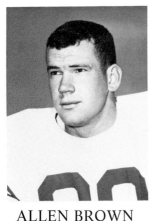
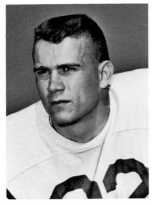

ALLEN BROWN
END   1964

BILL CLAY
HALF-BACK   1965

STAN HINDMAN
GUARD   1965

GLENN CANNON   ARCHIE MANNING
SAFETY   1969   QUARTERBACK   1969

INDEX OF NAMES

196 *Index*